RAILWAYS OF NORWICH

JOHN

IAN ALLAN Publishing

Right:
The approach to Thorpe in June 1984 as Class 47/0 No 47130 departs with the 10.43 service from Yarmouth to Birmingham New Street.
R. S. Freeman

Previous page:
A hybrid Cravens dmu, with 105/2 E51296 leading 141 No E56141 on the 17.53 to Ely.
Brian Morrison

First published 1994

ISBN 0 7110 2241 0

Designed by
David Collins

Published by Ian Allan Publishing

an imprint of Ian Allan Ltd, Terminal House, Station Approach, Shepperton, Surrey TW17 8AS; and printed by Ian Allan Printing Ltd, Coombelands House, Coombelands Lane, Addlestone, Weybridge, Surrey KT15 1HY.

Contents

Acknowledgement

I must acknowledge the help that I have received from a number of quarters, without which this book would have been impossible. D W. (Bill) Harvey and the late George Ewles gave an invaluable insight into the workings of the locomotive depot at Norwich. I have, as usual, used the Public Record Office at Kew, and it is always a pleasure to work there. Locally, staff at both the Norfolk Record Office and in the photo library at Eastern Counties Newspapers have been immensely helpful, and I am grateful to Malcolm O'Neill for his assistance with photography. All the people whose photographs appear in the book also deserve a vote of thanks, but especially Richard Adderson, whose willingness to loan material and supply information has been much appreciated. Above all, my thanks to my wife Wendy for putting up with me whilst compiling the whole thing!

Anyone who is interested in taking their study of Norwich and its railways further than this necessarily-brief account permits can join either or both of the relevant societies. The Great Eastern Society publishes a wide variety of material and meets regularly; its membership secretary is J. R. Tant, 9 Clare Road, Leytonstone, London E11 1JU. The society covers the system from its inception to the present day. The M&GN Circle caters for those interested in the Midland & Great Northern system generally, and its membership secretary is G. L. Kenworthy, 16 Beverley Road, Brundall, Norwich NR13 5QS. Again, the whole lifespan of the system is covered, and the Circle publishes a variety of material and holds meetings throughout the area. I can recommend both of them personally from long experience, and I would like to conclude by thanking officers and members of both organisations for all the work that they do.

Front cover top:
'Britannia' No 70030
William Wordsworth
is seen at Norwich Thorpe in
October 1960
Colour Rail

Front cover bottom:
At Norwich Thorpe on 18
July 1992 Class 47/0 No
47222 prepares to head for
Great Yarmouth with a
Regional Railways
Saturdays Only service from
Birmingham
Michael J. Collins

Back cover top:
The concourse at Thorpe in
the pre-electrification era
with first generation DMUs
prominent.
Brian Morrison

Back cover bottom:
On 30 August 1980 Class
47 No 47279 departs from
Norwich with the 08.00
service for Liverpool Street.
Hugh Ballantyne

Right:
A splendid Great Eastern-
era view of Norwich Thorpe,
taken in 1914 from platform
1/2, with a train loading in
platform 1, and another long
rake of 6 wheeled third-class
stock in No 3.
Locomotive & General

CHAPTER 1

The Early Years

A fine city, Norwich — and one which was the target for many railway schemes over the years. Early in the 19th century it was an important place, one of the few concentrations of population in an East Anglia very much noted for the scattered and impoverished nature of its inhabitants, and a major centre in the administrative, business and ecclesiastical worlds. It loomed large in the eyes of railway promoters.

The main line to Norwich can reasonably be said to have its origins back in 1834 when a prospectus for the 'Grand Eastern Counties Railway' was issued, although the 'Grand' was soon dropped. It was to have had a London terminus somewhere in the Shoreditch or Whitechapel area and would have followed the present line more or less exactly to Ipswich, and thence by a more easterly route to Norwich; had it been built, small, quiet country towns such as Debenham, Eye and Harleston might now seethe with commuters for London, rather than Stowmarket and Diss. The Bill received the Royal Assent on 4 July 1836, on the same day as that for the Northern & Eastern Railway which proposed to build to Cambridge, with a branch serving Thetford, Norwich and Yarmouth. At a very early stage this impoverished company approached the Eastern Counties with a view to sharing their Shoreditch terminus.

The line made rapid progress east of Stratford, and the first part to be opened was between Mile End and Romford, on 18 June 1839. The opening to Shoreditch took place on 1 July 1840, whilst at the same time it was extended to Brentwood at the country end. Colchester was not reached until almost three years later, the opening being on 29 March. It is a curious thing that when the line opened it was built to a track gauge of 5ft 0in, the Great Western having chosen 7ft $0^1/4$in; the Eastern Counties was way ahead of its illustrious contemporary in being converted to the standard gauge of 4ft $8^1/2$in in 1849.

The extension had not been without its problems, and the company found itself in serious financial difficulties, being rescued by a call upon its shareholders. Costs had been greatly in excess of those originally allowed, since the Essex clay and excessive rainfall in 1841 had seriously delayed construction. Meantime, associated lines were being opened in the London area and suburban traffic was growing rapidly.

The Eastern Counties showed no sign of being able to build its line to Yarmouth, although it retained an interest; it was with its agreement that the Yarmouth & Norwich Railway's bill was put through Parliament, receiving the Royal Assent on 18 June 1842. Yarmouth was then a fashionable watering place and the port for Norwich, and it was felt that the proposed line had good traffic prospects. With George Stephenson elected as Chairman of the company, and his son Robert as Engineer, the project was in illustrious hands, and work started in 1843. It proceeded rapidly, and the opening took place on 30 April 1844 with much celebration, bands playing the customary 'See the conquering hero comes'. Great banquets were consumed, and the line was notable for being

Previous page:
Class B17/1 No 1634
Hichingbrooke *enters the turntable at Norwich shed in 1947, the last year before the LNER passed into the hands of the nationalised British Railways*

V. C. Brown

the first in the country to be equipped with the Cooke & Wheatstone electric telegraph, a primitive forerunner of the block system. Norwich was at last on the railway map, the new terminus having two passenger platforms and two for goods, all on the site of the later Thorpe station.

The prospect of the original Eastern Counties line reaching Norwich still seemed no nearer. By 1845, surveying had reached Ardleigh for a proposed extension of the ECR main line from Colchester to Harwich, but parliamentary permission was refused. However the former Northern & Eastern line, now taken over by the Eastern Counties, was being extended from Bishop's Stortford to Newport and Brandon, and with an eye on its impending opening (it took place on 30 July 1845) thoughts in Norwich turned to linking with this line rather than to Colchester. The Norwich & Brandon bill duly received the Royal Assent on 10 May 1844, and Grissell & Peto were awarded the contract to build the new line, as they had already built the one from Yarmouth.

The only significant problem was that of crossing the River Wensum just outside the Norwich terminus, which was navigable at that point. It was necessary to design a bridge that could be opened so as to facilitate the passage of river traffic, and this led to the development of the first of the characteristic East Anglian swing bridges. The difficulties of this crossing were such that the line from Brandon was initially opened to the station at Trowse (on 30 July

Below :
A contemporary print from the opening of the present Thorpe station.
Norfolk Record Office

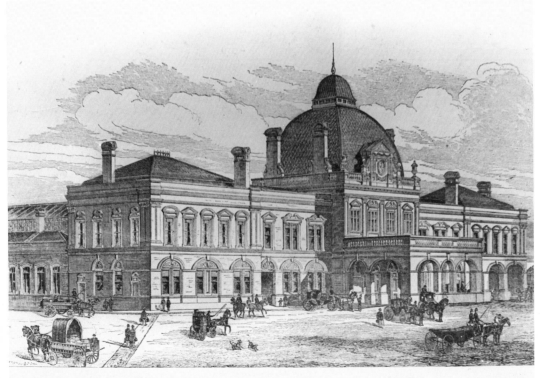

THE NEW RAILWAY STATION AT THORPE.

1845), the ceremonies having been on the previous day. The connection between Trowse and Thorpe Junction, on the Norwich & Yarmouth, finally opened on 15 December 1845. By this time, of course, the Norfolk Railway had come into being (on 30 June 1845) by the amalgamation of the Yarmouth & Norwich and Norwich & Brandon companies, the new company opening lines from Wymondham to Dereham on 7 December 1846 and Reedham to Lowestoft on 3 May 1847.

It became clear that the ECR line was not going to be extended beyond Colchester. The complete absence of Ipswich from the story so far had not gone unnoticed by the inhabitants of that town, who were aggrieved that arch-rival Norwich would soon have its own access to London. Accordingly the Eastern Union Railway was formed with the backing of the influential Cobbold family, and obtained its Bill for a line from Colchester to Ipswich on 19 July 1844. The route crossed three watersheds, the summits being near Parsons Heath, Ardleigh and Bentley, and at Manningtree it crossed the Stour estuary by two short viaducts. The line duly opened on 15 June 1846 — well behind Norwich — with all the usual ceremony. Goods traffic had been working over the line since 1 June, using locomotives that had arrived by sea from Messrs Sharp Bros.

On 21 July 1845 the Ipswich & Bury St Edmunds Railway obtained its Act, and although nominally independent, it was closely connected with the Eastern Union. The Act provided for the abandonment of the original Ipswich station and the building of one on the present site, northeast of Stoke Hill, together with the tunnel to connect the two lines. Construction of the line was relatively easy, and intermediate stations were provided at Blakenham (later Claydon), Needham, Stowmarket, Haughley, Elmswell and Thurston. The line opened on 7 December 1846, though all the stations were not ready, including the new one at Ipswich.

The next major event was the extension to Norwich. An Act for this was obtained by the Ipswich & Bury even before amalgamation with the Eastern Union, though it included provision for the purchase of all the parts by the EUR. The Eastern Counties, which had taken over the Norfolk Railway, feared abstraction of its traffic to London by the new route, and so would not permit it access to its terminus at Thorpe. This obliged the EUR to construct its own station in Victoria Street, and it had to cross the ECR line from Ely to reach it. Because of the likely increase in traffic, a bridge was required — Lakenham viaduct — rather than a crossing on the level, though it was also proposed to build a branch at Trowse to connect with the Eastern Counties line. Construction started at Lakenham on 25 February 1847, again with much celebration, since the new line offered Norwich a more direct route to London. Work also started between Haughley and Stowmarket. The new line opened in sections: to Finningham on 7 June 1848, Burston on 2 July 1849, and throughout on 7 November 1849, although after it had reached Burston, through passengers were taken on to Norwich by road. At the formal opening the usual ceremonies were observed, trains from Ipswich and Norwich uniting at Stowmarket, with travellers enjoying the usual repasts. Public traffic started quite some time after this, on 12 December, and goods traffic about two weeks later.

The connection between the Eastern Union and Eastern Counties, via what became known as Trowse Upper and Lower junctions, was opened on 27 August 1851. However, the Eastern Counties insisted that Eastern Union engines hauling exchange traffic should not enter on the ECR line, and so they had to run round their trains and propel their stock on to the main line. Other obstructive policies arose from the fact that the ECR was reluctant to see traffic diverted away from its route via Cambridge, and so embarked on a rate-cutting war, and tended generally to put obstacles in the way of through traffic: the service between Norwich and London via Ipswich was so bad as to be almost

Right:
The first station at Norwich was built for the Yarmouth & Norwich Railway, which opened in April 1844, with its frontage in Riverside Road. With the advent of the present station it was relegated to goods use.
Norfolk Record Office

unusable. However, the Eastern Counties took over the working of the Eastern Union and associated lines from 1 January 1854 by an arrangement legalised in an Act of 7 August of that year. This continued until 1 July 1862 when both were incorporated into the new Great Eastern Railway. The need for a separate station at Victoria had now gone, though its continued use for passengers was enforced in the Act allowing the takeover of the EUR by the ECR. Matters improved somewhat, and the GER gradually developed a reputation for smartness and efficiency with its blue-liveried locomotives and varnished-wood coaches, though it was never able to make the investments in service improvements of some of its more prosperous contemporaries.

The East Norfolk Railway provided one of the later links into Thorpe station on 20 October 1874 when it opened between Whitlingham Junction and North Walsham. The line finally opened through to Cromer on 26 March 1877, while the branch from Wroxham to Buxton (later extended to County School) was a later addition, in 1879; all of these were worked from the outset by the Great Eastern. Cromer and the North Norfolk coast being considered destinations of great potential, the Wensum curve was opened between Trowse Swing Bridge Junction and Wensum Junction on 1 October 1879, and this allowed the most important trains to avoid Thorpe station and run direct on to the East Norfolk route. Finally, in June 1883, the direct line to Yarmouth via Acle was opened, and Brundall became a junction.

The section of line between Thorpe and Brundall was the scene of one of Britain's worst railway accidents on the evening of 10 September 1874, when the 5pm Liverpool Street-Yarmouth express collided head-on with the 8.40pm up Mail, in heavy rain, between Whitlingham and the Yare bridge. Ironically, although the line was still single and worked by the five-needle Cooke & Wheatstone instruments inherited from the Norfolk Railway, the second track had been laid and was awaiting inspection by the Board of Trade. A series of blunders by staff at Thorpe station, coupled with a system quite inadequate for controlling traffic on a busy single line, led to the ghastly collision in which both engine crews and 21 other people died, and a further 73 were injured.

Accidents apart, the Great Eastern did not have things all its own way. Just as the Eastern Union had been born out of frustration with the Eastern Counties lines to Norwich, other eyes were being cast on the Norfolk traffic, especially from the direction of the Midlands. The Norwich & Spalding Railway obtained its Act in August 1853, although (despite its title) it was intended to build a line only from Spalding, through Holbeach, to Sutton Bridge, although an extension to Norwich was mooted. The first section opened, worked by the Great Northern, in 1858, and finally reached Sutton Bridge in July 1862. Meantime, other lines were being built, such as the Yarmouth & North Norfolk and the Lynn & Fakenham, and ultimately these were extended to make a new through route to the Norfolk coast. Part of this was formed from the Norwich extension of the L&F, authorised in its Act of 1880, which

Opposite page -bottom :
A superb shot of 0-6-0T
No 549 departing from
Norwich in the early years of
the 20th century.
Norfolk Record Office

Right:
A superb Great Eastern view of Thorpe station, on 9 April 1914, looking towards the buffers and the distinctive dome of the main building. There is a variety of passenger-rated traffic in evidence, such as the milk churns on platform 1, which also hosts a long train of horse boxes. The fine gas light on platforms 3/4 also supports the telegraph wires, and the bracket signal at the end of platform 5 has arms for both directions. There is, of course, no platform 6. The goods station is just about discernible behind the horse-boxes.
        Norfolk Record Office

Right:
Another in the fine series of official Great Eastern photographs, this time showing the frontage of Thorpe station, again taken on 9 April 1914. The motor car has made its appearance and has already supplanted the horse-drawn cabs. Gas remains supreme for lighting.
        Norfolk Record Office

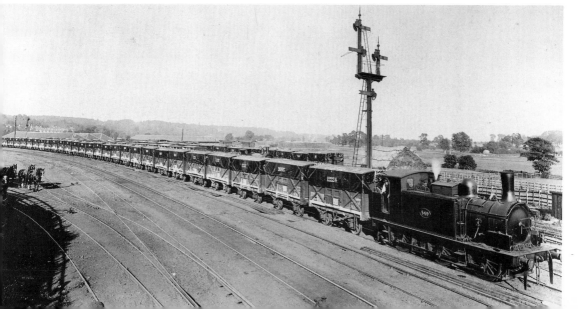

envisaged a line from Fakenham through Melton (now to be suffixed 'Constable'), Guestwick and Lenwade. The first section opened to Guestwick on 19 January 1882, passing Pigg's Grove summit, near Thursford, which was the highest point on what became the M&GN. The next $6^1/2$ miles to Lenwade opened on 1 July of that year, and the final $10^1/4$ miles to the new City station on 2 December 1882. There were also stations at Drayton and Hellesdon, and the new terminus, although incomplete, was opened with all the usual celebration, including a through train from King's Cross.

There had been other ambitions, of course, and even before the line was opened, plans were afoot to make the new line more convenient for the centre of Norwich. In spite of the tag 'City', the station was not particularly well-placed, and a plan deposited in 1880 outlined a scheme for a central station. This would have been reached by a line joining the proposed Lynn & Fakenham just to the west of the junction of the Aylsham and Fakenham turnpikes (the latter now the Drayton Road), which would have curved around the east side of the Castle, crossed Prince of Wales Road and terminated in King Street. Much property demolition would have been involved, and, needless to say, the scheme — and others like it — came to nothing.

Below :
Foundry Bridge over the River Wensum, leading to Prince of Wales Road, and with tram No 25 crossing. The gas lamps are mounted directly on to the trolley poles. Date unknown, but skirts have not yet risen above ankle level.
Norfolk Record Office

In a book about railways a brief mention needs to be made of trams. In Norwich the first steps were taken in the 1879 Parliamentary session for a series of connecting lines. Essentially they ran from the approach road to Whitlingham Junction station, along the Yarmouth turnpike and Thorpe Road to Foundry Bridge over the River Wensum outside Thorpe station, although there was no intention at that stage to run into the forecourt. The line then went along Prince of Wales Road, turning left at the Post Office into Castle Meadow, thence via Golden Ball Street, All Saints Green and Upper Surrey Street, right into Queens Road, eventually running into Heigham Road and Dereham Road, where it terminated at the junction with Workhouse Lane.

The system as built extended far beyond this, with the tracks radiating out along most of the main roads, and taking current from overhead lines. They went out to Eaton, along Dereham Road to its junction with Merton Road, passing the cemetery, Norwich Union workhouse and the hospital on the way. Another route went along Unthank Road to the Jenny Lind Hospital, at the junction of Mile End Road and Colman Road, now the old Ring Road. Another route went along City Road to Sunny Hill, another to Trowse station, and another up to the Pavilion on Mousehold Heath. There were car sheds in Ladysmith Road, approached from the Magdalen Road direction. One route passed the City station on its way out to the Aylsham Road, and although trams — later replaced by motor buses — looped into Thorpe station, Victoria probably had the best tram connections of the three stations, with a major intersection at the Queens Road-St Stephens crossroads. The system closed in 1935.

Below :
Streamlined 'B17' No 2870 City of London is pictured at Norwich Thorpe in May 1939. The two locomotives of the class that were selected for streamlining were painted in apple green and black livery. The standard 4,200gal tender was also modified. The duo were designed for use on the 'East Anglian' express service to London, and retained their streamlining until 1951.
J.P.Wilson

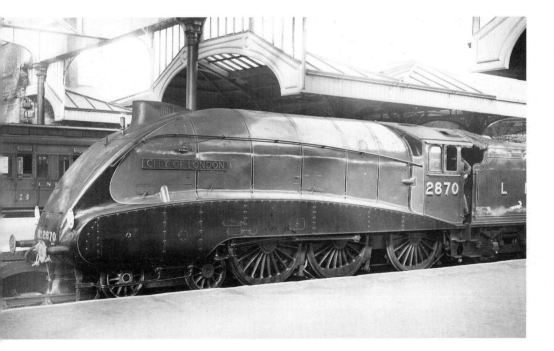

Above :
A dramatic composite panorama of Norwich Thorpe station in the early years of the 20th century.
   Norfolk Record Office

Right :
The centre of Norwich showing (top) City, (extreme right) Thorpe and (centre left) Victoria.
   Ordnance Survey;
   Crown Copyright
   Reserved

CHAPTER 2

The Midland & Great Northern

The next real development came with the amalgamation of the Lynn & Fakenham, Yarmouth & North Norfolk and Yarmouth Union Railways into the Eastern & Midlands, the first stage taking place on 1 January 1883. During the summer the Norwich line saw a service of seven trains each way, mostly through from Lynn. Other lines progressively came into the new company, and services started to develop, with two through trains daily between Cromer and King's Cross providing connections at Melton to and from Norwich from the summer of 1887. Severe financial difficulties developed, however, and the Eastern & Midlands went into receivership in June 1889. Litigation and general wrangling ensued all the while that the E&M was maintaining the service, and on 9 June 1893 the Midland & Great Northern committee was incorporated to take over the E&M. This joint ownership continued through the Grouping of 1923, the lines continuing to be referred to as the 'M&GN' although now owned by the LMS and LNER. Joint ownership continued until Nationalisation in 1948, although the LNER took over sole responsibility for the operation of the line in 1936.

By the 1920s the City station had become well-established, and the M&GN had managed to capture a significant proportion of the traffic to the Midlands. Norwich City saw a service of five stopping and two fast trains from Melton Constable, the fasts calling only at Drayton. In the other direction, the service was similar, although the 9.35am fast to Melton (which carried through coaches for the celebrated 'Leicester') called at Drayton only by request to pick up for Peterborough, Bourne and beyond, and the 3.15pm fast not at all. The 5.20pm stopper left at 5.30pm on Saturdays, but managed to reach Melton at the same time as on weekdays — 6.20pm. In 1920 a Sentinel Steam Coach had been tried out on local services on the line, but had not been successful.

The road approach to City was along Station Road, off Oak Street. Located on the west bank of the Wensum, a single track approached the station, crossing the river near Dolphin Bridge. There was a three-road engine shed, rebuilt in November 1927, and a turntable. The imposing building fronted a long platform with two outer faces of about 700ft each, with two shorter central bays between them of about 275ft. A siding from the east side of the layout crossed Station Road with a trailing connection into Westwick depot. Most of the site is now obliterated by the inner ring road.

World War 2 was not at all kind to the M&GN in Norwich. It had retained most of its train services — the 1942 timetable showed six trains each way daily, except Sundays. The station was hit in the heavy bombing of 1942, and on Monday night (27/28 April) the goods shed was severely damaged, and the goods offices and grain shed were burnt out. Some goods traffic was transferred to Thorpe station, but City reopened on 29 April. However, it was again hit by high explosive bombs on Wednesday night (29/30 April), and rail access was prevented, although services were restored by Thursday afternoon.

Previous page:
Passengers returned briefly to City on 21 May 1960 when the M&GN Joint Railway Preservation Society ran a tour covering Norwich and the remains of the Waveney Valley line. One of the engines, 'J15' No 65469, is here being watered. The other locomotive involved was the last 'B12', No 61572.

M&GN Circle

By the end of the war an extra train had already appeared. The 'Leicester' missed the lesser stations to and from Melton, and Hellesdon was also missed by the last trains out of Norwich on weekdays and Saturdays. DMUs appeared on local services from 18 September 1957, and they were increased to eight trains on Mondays-Fridays, with extras on Saturdays. The devastation of the war years was repaired, but it was a much smaller City station that emerged — gone was the imposing frontage, replaced by a modest flat-roofed single-storey building, a much-shortened awning clad with corrugated asbestos sheets, very much in the later LNER utilitarian style. Through workings increased, as on other parts of the system, with trains between Thorpe and City, one reversing at Cromer Beach. Goods traffic continued to be heavy, with City handling coal, roadstone and glass bottles — this continued for

The track plan of Norwich City in 1886.

Ordnance Survey; Crown Copyright Reserved

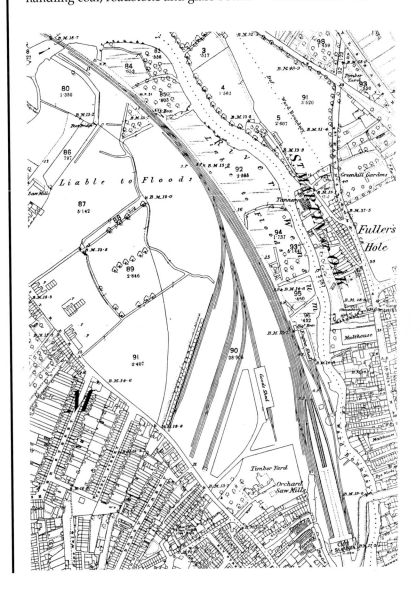

some time after closure to passengers. As elsewhere, local deliveries had been by horse-drawn wagons, and although these started to be replaced with motors in the 1920s, the process was not completed until about 1949.

Closure of the M&GN system has been well-chronicled elsewhere. The various economies were deemed by the authorities to be insufficient, and since it was in direct competition with the GER lines, it became the first of the wholesale closures, on 28 February 1959. The whole affair seems to have been dealt with in indecent haste. The Eastern Region of British Railways proposed the closure in September 1958, and it had been approved by the Area Committees of the TUCC by mid-November. The Central Transport Consultative Committee gave its approval on 25 November, and congratulated all concerned in sealing the fate of the M&GN in only 10 weeks! Norwich City was one of those places which retained its freight facilities, although for a time it was necessary to work traffic from Thorpe, a mile or so away as the crow flies — 61 miles by rail via Sheringham. Later the Themelthorpe curve was constructed, involving rebuilding the branch from Reepham. It finally closed officially on 3 February 1969, Drayton having gone in 1963 and Hellesdon in 1964, although the latter lost its passenger services as long ago as September 1952. The line was then cut back to Lenwade, which remained open for traffic from the Anglian Building Products works until the 1980s. The Wroxham-Aylsham section has subsequently been converted into the narrow gauge Bure Valley Railway.

Below :
City station is seen on 26 August 1912 in the great floods of that year, when much of East Anglia was inundated. Water has risen to the level of locomotive axles — several are 'on shed', and the track and yard are obstructed by timber and trees that have been washed up.
Norfolk Record Office

Right :
M&GN Railway No 98
reposes inside the shed at
Norwich City around 1934;
both locomotive and the
surroundings are
remarkably clean and tidy.
          M&GN Circle

Right :
In the platform at City,
where M&GN Railway
4-4-0 No 79 waits to go on
shed. Dated 23 September
1933, this could easily be a
pre-Grouping scene. Note
the Whittaker tablet
exchange apparatus on the
front of the tender.
          M&GN Circle

Right :
A fine panoramic view of
Norwich City, looking back
towards the station. The
main platforms are on the
outside, with two bays in the
centre; the signals are well
worth a second look, as is the
speed restriction board.
          A. G. Ellis Collection

20

Right :
Norwich City station suffered badly during World War 2, and a careful study of this photograph will show that the old building has gone, to be replaced with one much smaller — the new roof can just be seen behind the train. The water tank has lost its false panelling.

A. G. Ellis Collection

Below right:
City station, again seen looking towards the main building, but this time near to the canopies. Note the screens on the one behind the locomotive (No 32); also the insulators and telegraph wires attached to the top of the gas lamp.

A. G. Ellis Collection

Below :
Outside the front of the station three of the M&GN's horse-drawn delivery vehicles pose for the camera, together with their crews and motive power. Horses lasted here for this purpose until the late 1940s.

M&GN Circle

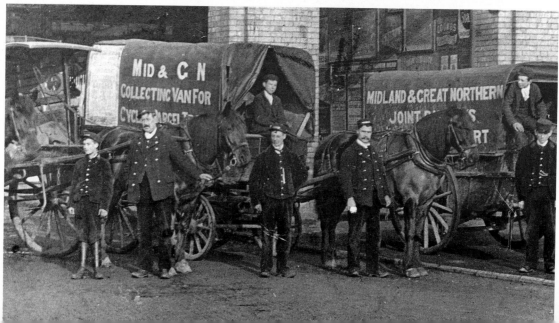

Right :
One of the main nameboards at Norwich City, beautifully illustrating the M&GN style. This lasted until the end — the photograph is dated 22 February 1959, a week before the passenger service finished.
M&GN Circle

Far right :
A fine view of the starting signals at City, showing to good advantage the M&GN's use of concrete for signal and guy posts.
M&GN Circle

Right :
In happier days members of the M&GN's Norwich City first-aid team pose on the platform with their trophies, plus some of their essential equipment — stretcher and portable case. Mr Bloxham is 5th from the left — does anyone know the others?
M&GN Circle

Right:
Passengers returned briefly to City on 21 May 1960 when the M&GN Joint Railway Preservation Society ran a tour covering Norwich and the remains of the Waveney Valley line. One of the engines, 'J15' No 65469, is here being watered. The other locomotive involved was the last 'B12', No 61572.
                    M&GN Circle

Right:
Drayton was the second call from Norwich on the line to Melton Constable, and one of the most important of the intermediate stations on the section. In this rather battered 1935 photograph Permanent Way trolley No 2 and some of the staff are posed at the end of the platform, with the signalbox and a tablet catcher in the background. The staff include stationmaster W. Brunning, signalman Vic Moy, and porters Cliff Holland and Ernest Beckett.
                    M&GN Circle

Right:
Track lifting has begun between Norwich and Drayton, and in these views, taken on 21 February 1973, it has reached the 'A frame' bridge outside City.
                    Eastern Counties
                    Newspapers

ght :
orwich City in 1928.
Ordnance Survey;

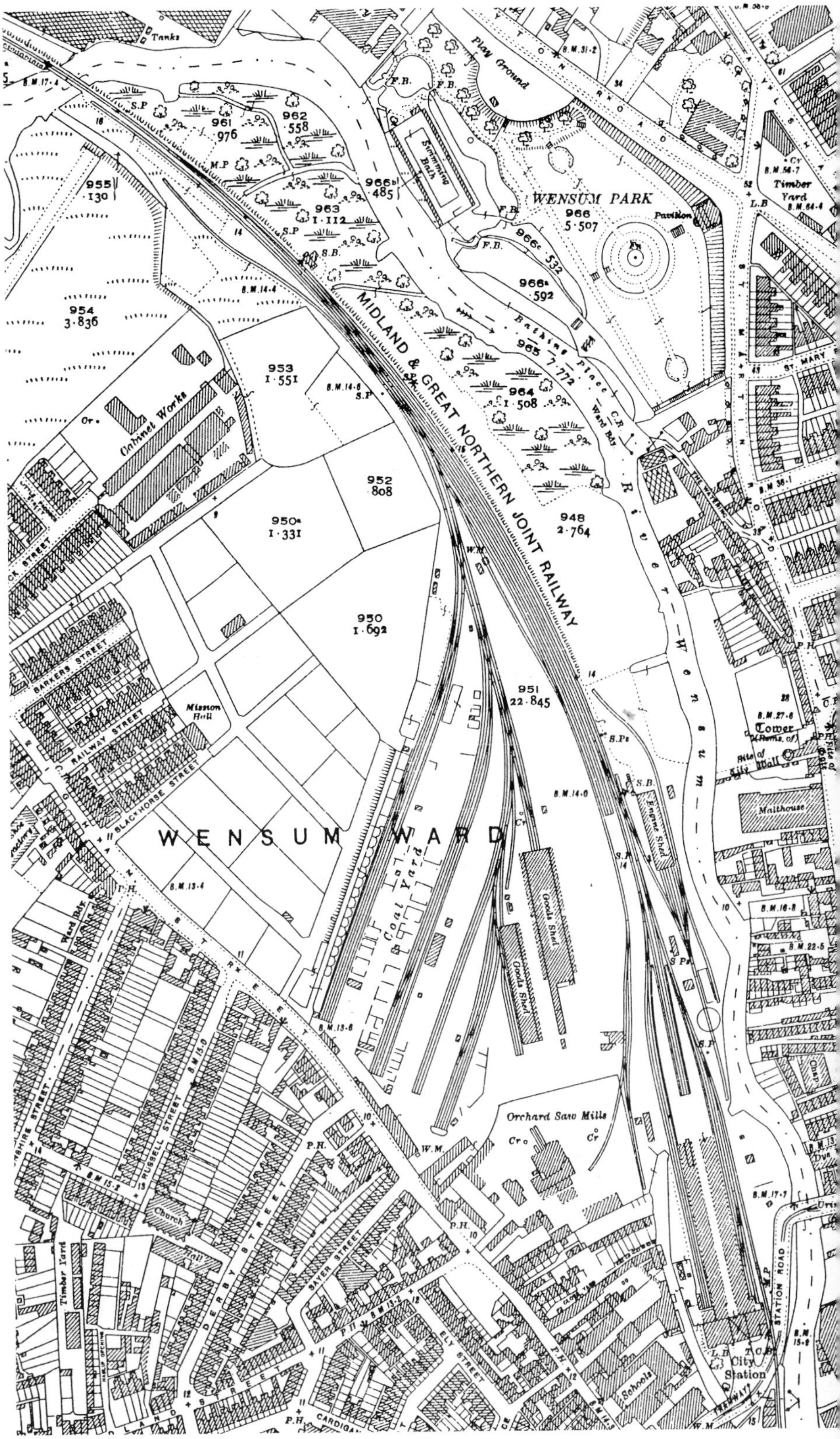

Table 51 — MELTON CONSTABLE, SHERINGHAM and CROMER

MONDAYS TO FRIDAYS

(timetable columns, am/pm services)

	Miles									
52 Norwich (City) .. dep										
Melton Constable .. dep										
5 Holt										
8½ Weybourne										
11½ Sheringham	arr / dep									
13 West Runton										
15 Cromer (Beach)	arr									
41¾ 46 Norwich (Thorpe) arr										

SATURDAYS ONLY

SATURDAYS ONLY—continued / **SUNDAYS**

MONDAYS TO FRIDAYS

	Miles						
46 Norwich (Thorpe) dep							
— Cromer (Beach) .... dep							
2 West Runton							
3½ Sheringham	arr / dep						
6½ Weybourne							
10 Holt							
— Melton Constable..	arr						
52 Norwich (City) arr							

SATURDAYS ONLY / **SUNS**

Notes (Table 51):
- **A** or † Second class only
- **B** Through Carriages from Leicester (London Road) (Table 50)
- **C** First and Second class
- **D** Until 6th September conveys Through Carriages from Derby (Mid.) (Table 50)
- **E** Arr 4 minutes earlier
- **F** Through Carriages to Derby (Mid.) (Table 50)
- **G** On Saturdays 14th and 21st June conveys Through Carriages to Birmingham (New Street) (Table 50)
- **H** Through Carriages to Shirebrook W. (Table 50)
- **J** Through Carriages to Leicester (London Road) (Table 50)
- **M** Through Train from Norwich (Thorpe). From 28th June to 6th September inclusive conveys Through Carriages to Peterborough (North)
- **N** Through Train to Norwich (Thorpe)
- **P** Runs 28th June to 23rd August inclusive
- **Q** Through Train from Fakenham (West)
- **R** Through Train from Norwich (City)
- **T** Through Carriages to or from Birmingham (New Street) (Table 50)
- **X** Through Train from Norwich (Thorpe)
- **Y** Through Carriages to or from London (Liverpool St.) (Table 46)
- **Z** Through Train to Norwich (City)

For OTHER TRAINS between Sheringham and Cromer and Norwich (Thorpe), see Table 46

Table 52 — MELTON CONSTABLE and NORWICH (City)

Second class only, except where otherwise shown

Week Days only

	Miles								
Melton Constable .. dep									
2 Hindolvestone									
4½ Guestwick									
8½ Whitwell and Reepham									
10½ Lenwade									
12½ Attlebridge									
16½ Drayton									
21½ Norwich (City) arr									

Week Days only

	Miles								
Norwich (City) .. dep									
5 Drayton									
9 Attlebridge									
11 Lenwade									
13 Whitwell and Reepham									
17 Guestwick									
19½ Hindolvestone									
21½ Melton Constable arr									

Notes (Table 52):
- **†** First and Second class
- **B** On Mondays to Fridays Through Train to Sheringham
- **C** Through Train from or to Cromer (Beach) (Table 51)
- **D** Through Train except Saturdays from Cromer (Beach). Saturdays only from Weybourne (Table 51)
- **F** Through Train to Weybourne arr 11 41 pm (Table 51)
- **G** On Saturdays Through Train to Cromer (Beach)
- **H** Through Train to Fakenham (West) arr 4 8 pm (Table 50)
- **J** Through Train to Fakenham (West) arr 6 40 pm (Table 50)
- **K** Through Train from Holt dep 7 48 am (Table 51)
- **P** Calls to set down passengers only
- **Q** Through Train from or to Sheringham

Table 53 — ESSENDINE and STAMFORD

Week Days only

	Miles								
Essendine .. dep									
1½ Ryhall									
4 Stamford Town.. arr									

Week Days only

	Miles								
Stamford Town .. dep									
2½ Ryhall									
4 Essendine .. arr									
92½ 2 London (King's C.)									

Notes (Table 53):
- **A** From 5th July to 30th August inclusive dep King's Cross 11 40 am
- **B** From 26th July until 16th August dep King's Cross 2 28 pm
- **E** Except Saturdays
- **S** Saturdays only
- **V** On Saturdays arr King's Cross 10 2 pm (9 10 pm from 19th July to 30th August)
- **†** Second class only

Above :
The Norwich City-Melton Constable timetable of the mid-1950s.

Opposite:
'J39' No 64968 meets 'D16/3' No 62515 at Whitwell & Reepham on 13 June 1957.
E. Tuddenham

Right:
A good general view of City and its train, again on 24 February 1959. There seems precious little traffic for the Scammel, and the barrows are bare with only a very few days left to closure.
Norfolk Record Office

CHAPTER 3

The Postwar Years

Wartime affected all railways, not least in the extra traffic which they had carried at almost no benefit to themselves in revenue terms. This had taken a heavy toll in wear-and-tear, as had the more obvious damage due to enemy action. Thorpe station was hit — Norwich as a whole suffered badly — and the LNER considered that much work needed to be done there and elsewhere. The finance was to come from a general 'war damage' claim, plus the budgets that would have been allocated to routine maintenance. In the list of 'first priority' projects drawn up in 1945 several new running loops were proposed, including one on the down side at Trowse Lower. General improvements were to be made at a cost of £25,000 to the locomotive depot at Thorpe, including additional ashpit facilities, washing out plant and additional stores. The goods facilities were to be restored and improved, the whole of the £68,000 cost coming from the War Damage claim. In the 'second priority' list were the provision of more and lengthened platforms, together with additional running lines to Thorpe Junction, at a cost of £55,000; additional carriage sidings, carriage washing plant, and a cleaning, inspection and maintenance shed, pre-heating plant and stores were also to be built at a cost of £191,000. The District Superintendent and District Locomotive Superintendent were to receive extended premises at a cost of £10,000. Little came of these schemes, although matters did eventually improve in the locomotive depot, and platform 6 was eventually built. Matters seemed to drag once Nationalisation came about, as the new British Railways organisation sorted out its priorities.

Below :
In with the new — the replacement buildings immediately after the war. A very few of the old stanchions and 'E&MR' (Eastern & Midlands Railway) spandrels have survived, but little else. The LNER poster board bears notice of the 1947 Transport Act nationalising the railways.

Locomotive & General

Right :
The end of steam was hastened along in Norwich by Kings scrapyard; condemned stock was often first held in the sidings at Trowse Lower. Standard Class 4 2-6-4T No 80013 awaits its fate in the yard in about 1965.
Dr Ian C. Allen

Right :
*Two Class A3 Pacifics —
Nos 60065* Knight of the Thistle *and 60091* Captain Cuttle *make their only visit to Norwich, standing in the sidings at Trowse Lower awaiting scrapping.*
Dr Ian C. Allen

Below :
An unidentified WD 2-8-0 shunts the sidings at Trowse Lower.
Dr Ian C. Allen

HACKNEY CARRIAGE STAND
FOR 10 CARRIAGES

Left:
A characteristic Great Eastern signalbox — Wensum Junction — photographed on 12 April 1969. It was taken out of use prior to the introduction of multiple-aspect signalling from Colchester, and rebuilt at Sheringham on the North Norfolk Railway.
Robert Humm Collection

Below left:
Hethersett was the first station out of Norwich on the line towards Thetford and Ely, and although closed for passengers in January 1964, and for general goods just over a year earlier, its signalbox survived until the MAS scheme was implemented.
Robert Humm Collection

Top right:
Whitlingham Junction was a station on the coast line out of Norwich, where the Cromer and Yarmouth lines diverged. It lost its passenger services in September 1955 and general goods nine years later, although it remained in use for private siding traffic for much longer. This view is taken from the footbridge (still in use) looking east along the derelict platforms.
Adrian Vaughan Collection

Centre right:
Whitlingham Junction, clearly showing the fine Great Eastern footbridge, retained because of the right-of-way over it, looking eastwards in about 1960.
Adrian Vaughan Collection

Right:
In this early 1950s view of Whitlingham Junction a goods train is being crossed over at the west end of the station. Coaches are being stored in the yard, many years later the site of a Portland Cement depot.
Douglas Thompson

Right:
A fine view of the old swing bridge at Trowse, taken in 1984, with the signalbox in the background and Crown Point depot just visible on the right. The Wensum curve once swung off to the right at the box, allowing express trains to the coast to avoid Thorpe station.
Adrian Vaughan
Collection

Right:
Trowse station closed to passengers in 1939, but its yards remained vital for goods traffic. Trowse Lower junction signalbox is hidden by the bridge; Trowse Yard box is not far behind the camera. The flint buildings are most unusual in their style and still exist. The centre platform was not demolished until 1987, serving passengers for the last time when the station temporarily reopened as the throat at Norwich Thorpe station was remodelled in 1986.
Author's Collection

Right:
Class J39 No 64731 departs from Norwich Thorpe with a goods train on 6 August 1958. Brush No D5513 stands at the fuelling point.
F. Church

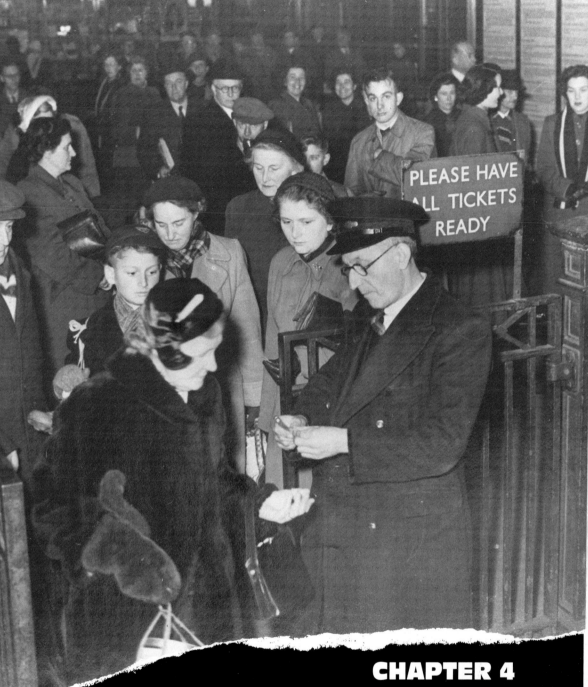

PLEASE HAVE
ALL TICKETS
READY

CHAPTER 4

Thorpe Station

The original Thorpe passenger station (it acquired the name when Victoria opened) had two platforms, each with its own roof, and with brick buildings adorned by an Italianate tower on the Riverside Road frontage. When the Norwich & Brandon line opened, the yard was extended, and as new lines brought more traffic, the need for ever-larger facilities became pressing. The present-day passenger station opened 'for public inspection' on 1 May 1886, and for traffic two days later. The original was then turned over to goods usage, and was hit by bombs in World War 2, necessitating work continuing entirely out in the open for a time.

The new building, a lofty structure in red brick with white Bath stone dressing, cost £60,000 and featured a fine dome with a covered colonnaded approach for carriages. The main concourse was covered by a very high roof supported on massive pillars and steelwork, with much ornamentation on some of the supporting brackets. Canopies extended along the platforms providing considerable shelter; platform 1 was screened from the adjacent goods depot by a brick wall. For many years the forecourt was used as a tram terminus, and after trams finished became the bus station. Refurbishment work took place in 1953 when a new ticket, seat reservation and enquiry office was provided at a cost of £8,000. The forecourt was also modified by removal of the long-redundant tram lines and was laid out as a car park. By this time the station was issuing 500,000 tickets annually (including 5,000 seasons), and 20,000 seat reservations; things looked promising with the Great Eastern main line still high in the 'fastest trains' league with the 'Broadsman' covering the 46.3 miles from Ipswich in 44min, an average of 63.1mph. Further reconstruction of the station waiting rooms occurred in 1957.

There were carriage sidings (now used for stabling of DMUs) next to platform 6, and at the end nearest the buffers, set into the bank was the train control office. Next to platform 1 was a bay known as the 'Royal dock', not for its use by Kings and Queens but because the Royal Mail was loaded there. The engine for the 9pm goods from Norwich, usually a 'J15', would set back into the dock and pick up a van with travelling postmen. This would then be attached to the front of the forty or more wagons of the goods, and conveyed mail for Diss, Stowmarket and Ipswich which was sorted en route.

The area between the tracks going into the passenger and goods stations was occupied by Thorpe Station signalbox (which appeared on the plans as 'Passenger Yard Signal Box') and the 70ft turntable, installed in 1936 to replace a smaller one. This was vacuum-operated, and all that was needed was for the engine to be run onto it, connect up the pipes and simply 'blow it round'. Close by was the single-storey brick staff accommodation block, which housed oil and tool stores, a report room where drivers filled in details of engine defects and the like, the fitters' mess, cleaners' mess and the drivers' and firemen's mess. Across the tracks into the goods depot was the Goods Yard signalbox. The depot had extensive facilities as befitted a city of Norwich's importance. The

Previous page:
One of the most important jobs on the railway was the checking of tickets here being done on the barrier at Thorpe in 1953.

Eastern Counties
Newspapers

Below:
Remnants of the tram lines into the forecourt of Thorpe Station were finally lifted in November 1955, together with the old stone setts, prior to remodelling of the area. British Railways lorries and vans, including a four-wheeled tractor unit, an AA motor-cycle patrolman and a rear-platform Eastern Counties bus complete the scene looking towards Foundry Bridge. Compare this with photograph on page 12.

Eastern Counties
Newspapers

shed boasted three covered platforms, served by tracks joined in the conventional manner, but also having another running across its mouth at right angles, and connected by a series of wagon turntables. A separate structure covered a further two tracks, and allowed direct loading or unloading between rail and road vehicles. Messrs. Rowntrees and Lyons had depots; Shell-Mex and Charringtons had rail-served oil terminals, and Boulton & Paul's private siding handled large quantities of raw materials and finished products from their joinery works; there were the usual coal merchants, including Messrs A. Dawnay and H. Parker.

The Norwich area had been a heavy user of containers for freight for many years, much traffic being associated with the Birds Eye factories on the coast. Originating goods also included boots, shoes, electrical appliances and Colman's many products including mustard, Robinsons cordials and Wincarnis wines. Much seasonal traffic passed through Norwich and created its own demands on the loco depot. Whilst the summer saw very heavy passenger traffic to and from the coastal resorts, extra trains had to be run in the spring to carry fruit and vegetables, and there were heavy express fish workings during the autumn herring season.

Above left:
A little later and the need for car parking is making itself felt, although the bus shelters are still in use. The ready-mixed concrete era has arrived, however.
> Eastern Counties
> Newspapers

Below left:
A busy but undated scene at Thorpe station in the late 1940s or early 1950s. Crowds throng on to platform 4 for a London train, and No 5 is jammed with passengers, possibly for Yarmouth.
> Eastern Counties
> Newspapers

Right:
Times change, and with some of the new standard BR coaches in the background, the Norwich Thorpe Civil Engineer's gang pose for the camera on 19 October 1967. The occasion was the introduction of high-visibility clothing; lookout man Bob Poll is wearing the new issue minivest.
> Eastern Counties
> Newspapers

Centre right:
Meantime, three booking clerks are hard at work in the booking office, where Edmondson cards and knuckle-punch dating presses are still the order of the day; 7 September 1965.
> Eastern Counties
> Newspapers

Bottom right:
Many people will have memories of National Service. Here, troops wait for transport on platforms 3 and 4 in 1956.
> Eastern Counties
> Newspapers

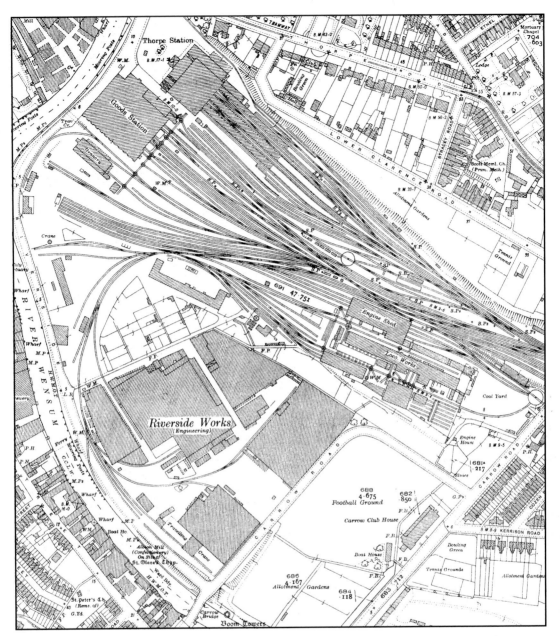

Above left:
The new era in practice in Thorpe station on 11 September 1963. On the left is English-Electric Type 4 No D209 at the head of the 1.40pm to Liverpool Street, whilst on the right Brush Type 2 No D5537 waits with an excursion to the speedway at Wembley Hill.

S. Creer

Left:
Inside Thorpe station multiple-units predominate. Although the photograph is undated, the flares must give some clue.

Eastern Counties Newspapers

Above:
Norwich Thorpe c1935.
Ordnance Survey; Crown Copyright Reserved

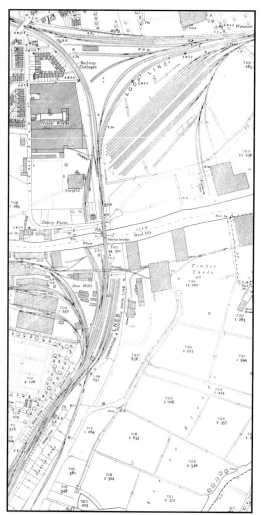

Above:
The Norwich Trowse/Trowse
swing bridge area c1928.
  Ordnance Survey; Crown
    Copyright Reserved

Right:
The LNER approaches to
Norwich in c1928.
  Ordnance Survey; Crown
    Copyright Reserved

CHAPTER 5

Norwich Shed

T he western end of the layout was bounded by Riverside Road, separating it from the Wensum, and at the other end was the somewhat tortuous Carrow Road. Located here was the ex-Great Eastern locomotive shed. Close by Bridge 357 was the 55ft hand-operated turntable, a survivor from an earlier era. It could not handle the new 'Britannias', although the '1500s' could be turned, provided that the balance was exactly right. Engines frequently got stuck, and the crew would then have to summon three or four of their mates to give an extra push. This table connected with the coaling plant, whose huge concrete tower dominated the skyline of Norwich depot, and had been built in 1936. Prior to this there had been an affair of staging: coal trucks would be run up the bank behind it and their contents shovelled out, and then into tubs on rails, which would be run up to the locomotive and tipped. At least four men had been permanently employed on this coaling stage.

Locomotive coal arrived by the trainload from Whitemoor in two classes: ordinary for goods engines, and best for passenger work. Wagons were stored on sidings by the coaling plant, and when required, one would be hauled up the side of the tower and its contents tipped bodily into the hopper. This also had the effect of tipping the oil out of the axle-boxes, so they had to be carefully checked and topped up after a visit to the plant. The hopper held about 250-300 tons of coal, which was enough to last through a day and the following morning. Coaling a locomotive involved positioning it under the plant, and the driver getting up via steps into the small control room. There was a movable chute which could be positioned appropriately for the particular engine; the driver then operated the electrical controls which activated a slide, which released the coal into the chute. It took about four minutes to coal a locomotive using the plant, which was demolished in 1963.

The locomotive depot at Norwich had started with the arrival of the Yarmouth & Norwich Railway. They constructed a long, low brick building with square central section and water tower over, and a four-road engine shed, and this remained until the depot finally closed with the transfer to Crown Point in the 1980s. The District Mechanical Engineer's office and ambulance room joined on at the southeast corner of this original structure. Another track coming from the depot turntable separated this from the shops: fitting, smithy and machine, and in Yarmouth & Norwich days this had also included the erecting shop. It had eight transverse pits, each with its corresponding doors; the overhead crane survived to the closure of the depot. For many years Norwich handled main works overhauls with the exception of new fireboxes, but this capability was downgraded in the 1930s. Later, when it became necessary to do heavier work on the 'Britannias' than was officially deemed possible, tools seemed to appear from various holes where they had lain hidden: Norwich and its men rose to the latest challenge.

The water softening plant with its great upright cylinder was at the eastern end of this complex. Water was supplied to the site via a dyke from the river, which led into the reservoir from where it

Previous page:
A tender engine on the small turntable, this time Class J15 No 65469 in March 1960. The locomotive has a tender weatherboard and is sheeted against the rain as it is turned by hand. This required considerable skill by the driver to balance it exactly.

John C. Baker

was pumped into the softener, a tall structure which removed the lime. Adjacent to this naturally enough were the sludge pits, formed with earth banks. After a few weeks in there the residues would set, and being mostly lime much of it was sold to farmers for spreading on their fields. A particular problem would arise when Boulton & Paul were galvanising and let the effluent run into the dyke, which caused the water to develop a thick foamy head looking rather like Guinness. The engines would then prime very badly, having to be run with no more than a quarter glass of water; even under normal circumstances and with treatment, they had to be washed out at least once a week because of the state of the water supply.

The various messes were at one end of the shops complex, each grade having its separate facilities. Beyond the softening plant and separated by another turntable road was the three-road engine repair shop, and the road motor engineer's depot, with the new canteen building in the angle formed by one of the doglegs in Carrow Road. It replaced all the former messes, and was for all grades. The running foreman's office was also there, and remained even after the opening of the new Crown Point depot. The timber yard and store adjoined this area, and in later years the new three-road diesel maintenance shed was built there.

In 1945, when the 'B1s' (Nos 1042-52, with Nos 1040/1 spare) had been allocated to Norwich, some had been single-crewed only. Sid Tallant, for example, had No 1042. This meant that they went to London and back with the regular crew, and then either sat around doing nothing, or went with another set of men to Whitemoor and back — or similar — which rather defeated the object of having regular crews. This was changed to double-manning about 1949.

From early in 1947, the renowned D. W. (Bill) Harvey took over as shedmaster at Norwich, leaving only when steam finally departed in 1962. He had had long experience of a variety of depots, both on the LNER and in Nigeria, and moved to Norwich from the post of mechanical foreman at Cambridge. His long stay allowed a continuity of policy, which was lacking at some of the places regarded as training depots, such as Ipswich or Melton Constable, where men would remain in charge only a short time before moving on. He was very well liked and respected by the men under him, and he was especially skilled in matters relating to valves and their setting. He had much to do with the new 'Planned Servicing System' instituted in 1948 by L. P. Parker, Motive Power Superintendent first of the Eastern Section of the LNER's Southern Area, and later — after Nationalisation — of the Western Section as well.

After Nationalisation it seemed to Bill Harvey that there was more paper and more committees. At Norwich these included the LDC (local district committee, involving footplate staff), workshop staff committees; two carriage & wagon committees (one for conciliation grades, the other for workshop grades); canteen committee; meetings with Plant & Machinery representatives (no committee) and road motor staff. There were debates about rosters and turns of duty, and a great deal of time was spent on committees, and very little (seemingly) on 'real' work!

In 1958 there were about 400 enginemen at Norwich, and about 100 mechanical and workshop staff, including labourers. The traffic manager was responsible for all of these, and for the carriage & wagon and outdoor staff including the wheeltapper (examiner), who might be called out to carry out repairs to vehicles in transit, for example to a hot box. He was also responsible for the Plant & Machinery section, which covered items such as the turntable, coaler and water softener, and the running repairs section of the

Above:
The original locomotive facilities were provided by the Yarmouth & Norwich Railway, and remained in use until the opening of the new depot at Crown Point. Here the view is from the sheds towards the diesel fuelling point by the Carrow Road bridge.
Adrian Vaughan

Above:
Looking towards the Yarmouth & Norwich Railway's original offices on 31 March 1985, after they had been abandoned for Crown Point.

Adrian Vaughan

Right:
The coaling tower at Norwich replaced a manual stage which had employed a considerable number of men simply shovelling all day, and brought the time for coaling an engine down to about four minutes.
                    M&GN Circle

Below:
Class J67/1 No 68516 is turned on the small ('shed') table, tucked away under the Carrow Road embankment at Norwich some time in 1958.

    Dr Ian C. Allen

Road Motor department. The total staff numbered 796.

Norwich had a number of pilot engines. The Crown Point pilot was a three-shift duty (6am, 2pm and 10pm), and so worked round the clock. It was available for transfer trips to Thorpe or Trowse yards, but was mainly concerned with shunting its own yard. Long-distance freight trains would arrive from Whitemoor with items such as bricks, coal and general merchandise, which would be re-formed into local goods trains for Lowestoft, Yarmouth and Cromer, and also for the 'round the world' line from Wroxham to Dereham. There were two pilots at Thorpe, one operating continuously for yard shunting, and the other on two shifts for Boulton & Paul's siding and shunting the coal ground. The Trowse pilot dealt with traffic for Wymondham and Wells, Beccles via the Waveney Valley, and with cattle. This latter was important on Saturdays when up to three trains could be run to London following the sales. A Norwich crew would work 35 trucks with a six-coupled engine to Stratford, lodge, and return with the empties. These would then be cleaned and disinfected, and stored at Trowse ready for the next Saturday, though they might be used during the week for the carriage of other livestock such as pigs from Acle, where Harry Pointer was the main dealer, and the sale on a Thursday. Alternatively, a local station might ring up for a few trucks for a consignment.

Many trains conveyed horse boxes, which were passenger-rated, and stations such as Foulsham, Aylsham or Dereham would attach them to local trains. This often happened on Saturdays, and on arrival in Norwich, they would be detached by the passenger pilot. This was also kept busy forming and re-forming trains, since numbers of them conveyed through coaches to places such as Yarmouth or Cromer.

Right:
The shed turntable again sees a 'J15', and is attracting considerable attention from various quarters as a snowplough is tried out.
Eastern Counties Newspapers

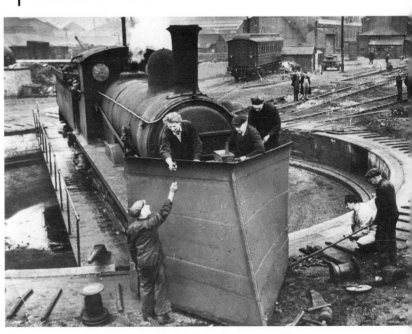

Right:
Two Class J67s, with
No 68633 nearest the
camera, stand by the large
('station') turntable at
Thorpe.
                Dr Ian C. Allen

Right:
'J15' No 65469 is turned on
the shed table at Norwich on
a rainy day in March 1960.
Note the extensive cycle
sheds, the new canteen and
the floodlights of Carrow
Road football ground.
                John C. Baker

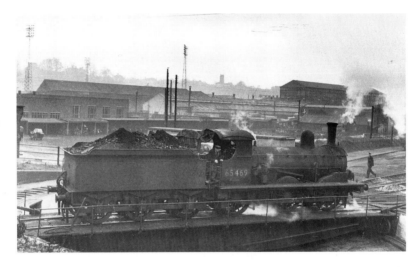

Right:
A thick smoky haze hangs
over Thorpe depot as engines
are prepared for work. The
coaling tower dominates the
scene; the end of the old
Yarmouth & Norwich
building is on the extreme
left. The picture is taken
from the small turntable at
the Carrow Road end.
                H. N. James

Right:
'J19' No 64674 and an unidentified 'K3' are in the depot at Norwich, with the turntable on one side and the coaler on the other.
Dr Ian C. Allen

Right:
The old depot was abandoned with the opening of the new one at Crown Point. Transfer is imminent in this 1984 view, in which the water tank looks forlorn, as do the oil and tool stores in the foreground.
Adrian Vaughan
Collection

Right:
Visitors approaching the depot from Carrow Road came first to the machine shops and smithy, which takes up most of this view. The portion in the left background was the fitting shop.
Adrian Vaughan
Collection

Right:
Looking towards the city
through and past the engine
shed, with the Goods Yard
signalbox also in view.
Adrian Vaughan

Right:
Class D16/3 No 62564 is
seen at Norwich — its home
depot — on 23 July 1955.
R. E. Vincent

Right:
Looking north, towards the city, this view of the new Crown Point maintenance depot shows the scale of the new installation.

British Rail

Right:
Whilst the electrification programme led to the abolition of the traditional signalboxes on the main line, the small new control panel at Crown Point was to remain. It is seen here on 16 March 1988.

Brian Morrison

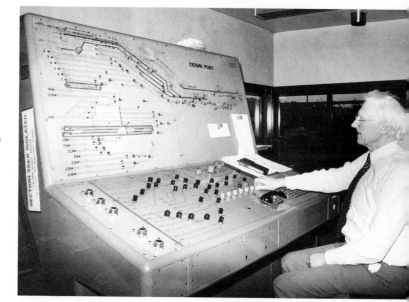

Right:
The interior of the carriage maintenance and servicing shed showing the cleaning platform and underfloor inspection pit. The depot also handled both locomotives and DMUs.

British Rail

CHAPTER 6

Victoria Station

Previous page:
The interior of Victoria station, in 1914, showing to fine effect the roof of the rotunda, a former circus building taken over by the Eastern Union Railway for its new terminus. Adverts for the Daily Sketch adorn the newspaper stall and railway posters extol the virtues of Great Yarmouth. This is a Great Eastern Railway official photograph.
Norfolk Record Office

As already mentioned, Victoria station was a relatively early casualty as services were transferred to Thorpe. It was, however, to survive until electrification as a freight terminal.

The Victoria pilot was booked to leave the loco depot as a light engine at 4.30am on weekdays and run to Trowse, where it would pick up the wagons for Victoria. If there were more than about 30 of these it might require banking as far as Trowse Upper junction by the Trowse pilot; the train would then be backed into Victoria. The pilot was then booked as being available for shunting from 6.15am 'till done'. The station dealt with coal — about a trainload a day — and general merchandise. Working between Trowse Yard or Thorpe and Victoria required reversal at Trowse Upper junction. Since coal arrived via the Thetford line, trains would have an engine attached in the rear and be drawn back past Trowse Lower to Upper, where the train engine would take it over the crossover and down the branch. It was quite possible to see a 'Britannia' being dragged back up from Trowse on such a working.

Victoria retained much of the appearance of a passenger station almost to the end. The main building, though small, had an imposing enough entrance with its three tall arches and nameboard over them, though the effect was spoiled by the cycle shed and odd bits of woodwork. What would have been the train shed over the platform was wooden and covered with corrugated sheeting, and was used for the loading and unloading of wagons. A brick water tower topped by an iron tank fed a column off the platform end,

Left:
Norwich Victoria station, seen from the forecourt again in 1914. The train shed can be seen on the extreme left, and the dome of the main building is just visible behind the transverse roof. This is a Great Eastern Railway official photograph.
Norfolk Record Office

Above:
Norwich Victoria in 1958, showing the signalbox, and much evidence of cement and coal traffic.
Adrian Vaughan
Collection

and to one side stood the goods shed, and then the coal roads. The approach from Trowse Upper was singled in June 1953.

The station survived as one of the goods yards for Norwich through into diesel days, continuing to handle bulk traffics such as cement, and was eventually converted for use as a coal concentration depot, with modern equipment for the unloading of coal from bottom-discharge hoppers. Its demise came about with the 1980s electrification scheme and the associated track rationalisation. The erstwhile junction and crossover at Trowse Upper were abolished, to be replaced with plain track, and it thus became possible to release the valuable city centre site for redevelopment. The passenger station had, in fact, become a car park, while the main coal depot was back beyond the Grove Road bridge which still exists, and is now a Sainsbury's supermarket.

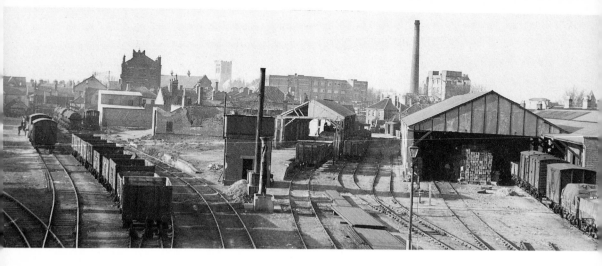

Above:
A view of the facilities at Norwich Victoria in 1948 showing the variety of traffic handled at this date.
　　　　　Real Photographs

Below right:
Much activity at Victoria in mid-1986 as No 08250 shunts its stock. There must be some track under there somewhere!
　　　　　R. J. Adderson

Far right:
Trowse Upper Junction was important right up to the resignalling for electrification, giving access to Norwich Victoria. Trains from Trowse Yard or cross-country would have been dragged backwards up to this junction, the crossover reversed, and the train engine would then have taken its load into Victoria. The signal is off for a down train to continue to Trowse Lower junction.
　Adrian Vaughan Collection

56

Right:
Norwich Victoria c1935;
notice the adjacent tram
tracks.

Ordnance Survey;
Crown Copyright
Reserved

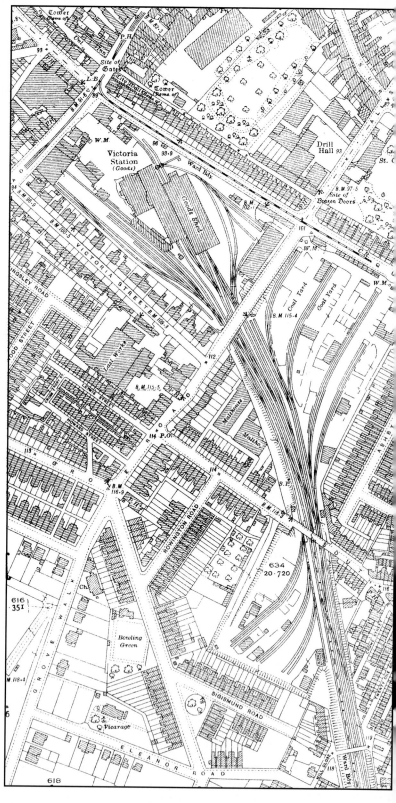

CHAPTER 7

Locomotives and Men

M

any men made their careers on the railway, living and working all their lives in one place. George Ewles was a Norfolk man born and bred, who ran away from school aged 12¹/₂ to work on a farm near home at Coltishall. There he saw trains on the Great Eastern's Wroxham to County School line, usually hauled by 'Intermediates' (later LNER Class E4) and determined to drive one some day. He started on 10 January 1919 at age 16 with the Great Eastern at Norwich Thorpe, and transferred in 1923 to Stratford as a fireman, starting in No 1 yard and moving later to No 2. He returned to Norwich in December 1925, and was made up to driver after about 10 years. Their rate of pay in the 1920s and 30s was £4.10s (£4.50) for a 48hr week, whilst the fireman's rate was £3.18s (£3.90). Sundays were paid at time-and-a-half, with time-and-a-quarter from 10pm to 4am. When the 'Britannias' left Norwich in 1962 he transferred to the English Electric diesels after giving up No 70013 *Oliver Cromwell* as his regular locomotive.

George Ewles finished driving on multiple units, and retired on 30 September 1966 aged 63¹/₂ years, and with 47¹/₂ of them on the railway. He had reluctantly taken early retirement, as it was the policy at this time to encourage younger staff. Geoffrey Ford was the superintendent at Norwich at the time, and saw George in his last week, telling him that he had a completely clean record; they shook hands. He put the record down to a lot of luck — not getting caught for some of the things that did happen!

Bob King, a driver at Norwich when George Ewles was still a cleaner, had regularly had 'B12' No 1509, and recalled how passengers would congratulate him on a perfect right-time arrival at Liverpool Street, saying that his chest swelled with pride. He would oil up No 1509 after he had finished his day's work if he were not working the following day, so that even if tomorrow's crew did no oiling at all, she would still be all right, and he always insisted on throwing the smokebox ash out himself, which could amount to as much as 20-30 barrowloads. It was important not to trap any ash at all in the door seal, otherwise it was not airtight; air could then be drawn in whilst running, causing overheating, and engines with this problem occasionally ran into Norwich with the smokebox door glowing red to the handles!

The 'Sandringhams' were three-cylinder 4-6-0s which could reach 80mph, but tended to roll, especially when they were about 18 months out of the shops. In 1935 two of the class were streamlined to work the 'East Anglian', Nos 2859 *East Anglian* and 2870 *City of London*. This train was latterly allowed two hours exactly between Norwich and London, with a two-minute stop at Ipswich. Four men were regularly allocated to these engines; No 2870 was always considered to be faster than No 2859. George Ewles was firing No 2870 on one occasion in World War 2, and noticed that the middle small end was using a lot of oil. The engine had almost completed 100,000 miles since being shopped, and was thus due for major overhaul, but had not once been stopped for repair in that time. It was a matter of great pride to the shed staff to get it past the 100,000 mark to achieve the remarkable

Previous page:
In May 1952 No 61572 stands in platform 5 at Thorpe station ready to work its train to the Norfolk coast. It looks very smart for a 50-year-old veteran.
John C. Baker

record, so on this occasion George got under the engine at Liverpool Street and oiled it up, and the mileage was safely achieved.

The 'Britannias' represented the climax of steam power on the Great Eastern. Their introduction en masse was largely due to the vision of Gerard Fiennes, then Assistant Superintendent at Liverpool Street. Together with Stuart Ward he constructed the new regular-interval timetable around their 32,000lb of tractive effort, requiring them to get from Norwich to Liverpool Street in just over two hours, calling only at Ipswich, and to make the return trip twice a day. Twenty three of the new locomotives were allocated to the Great Eastern section from new in 1951, and in spite of teething troubles settled down to give some sterling performances. They even gave the Great Eastern section Britain's fastest scheduled timings for a brief but glorious period!

At Norwich shedmaster Bill Harvey was especially interested in the 'Britannias' for two reasons: they were the first of the new national types of locomotive, and they were coming to East Anglia. Nos 70000-5 were allocated to Stratford, and the Norwich contingent arrived in May 1951, with 10 of them staying 10 years. He realised that the spotlight was on Norwich, and that questions might even be asked in the Houses of Parliament about these engines! He wanted to put on a good show, and in this he certainly succeeded handsomely. They had 25% more power than a 'B1', with a grate area 50% bigger, and they could handle trains much better than the smaller engines which they replaced whilst burning poorer-quality coal.

The traffic management organisation meant that the Norwich

Below:
In 1965 LNER Class V2 No 4771 Green Arrow stands outside the sheds at Norwich, whilst retired shedmaster Bill Harvey looks on.
Dr Ian C. Allen

'Britannias' went all over the country. In later years Stratford was often in trouble, and if one of theirs failed, Bill Harvey had to supply another, which was returned only when a washout was needed. Eventually conditions became so bad at Stratford that all the 'Britannia' allocation and maintenance in East Anglia was transferred to Norwich, making a total of 23 engines, although this was down to 16 by the early 1960s. Bill Harvey kept a close check on the movements of his 'Britannias', virtually becoming his own controller. He might find out from Control, for example, that one of his engines had been stopped at Sheffield, and would then be able to get it back quickly, and he thus kept their availability high. The 'Britannias' averaged about 7,000 miles per month, though No 70012 *Hotspur* once did over 10,000 miles in successive months. A double London trip (via Colchester) was 460 miles per day; one return trip via Cambridge was 264 miles.

Experienced drivers would swap with their mates and take a turn on the shovel: it kept them fit, and allowed the fireman to learn the road, the signal placings, and the techniques of driving, though Inspectors would reprimand crews if they found them changed over. It was, of course, the only way that firemen could learn to become drivers! A 'Britannia' could get 11 coaches from Norwich to Liverpool Street without trouble in two hours when the need arose, and though the trip could be done with one tank of water, it was customary to take it at the troughs at Ipswich. It was also common for a crew to work a train from Norwich out via Ipswich and back via Cambridge, or vice versa. Each locomotive was allocated to two drivers: from Norwich, one would take it to Liverpool Street and back in the morning, and the other in the afternoon. No 70007 *Coeur de Lion* was George Ewles' first regular 'Britannia', and was followed by No 70013 *Oliver Cromwell*. Later, a pair of small hooks was fitted on the cab side, and each driver given an engraved nameplate to hang there, so that the public knew who was in charge. As Driver Ewles said: 'When a man reached this position, he didn't think so much that he worked for the railway, he was so proud he thought he owned it!' The practice was continued into the early days of the new diesels, but didn't persist for long.

One of Bill Harvey's favourite Norwich engines had been 'B12' No 1572, which he kept in immaculate condition. In later days Stratford kept requesting its transfer for scrapping, but some excuse was always found why it could not go. Finally it did work up to London, but with strict instructions not to let it get to Stratford, and it escaped again. At last Bill had to take his annual leave, whereupon Stratford summoned No 1572, and it had gone when he returned. Fortunately it subsequently found its way to the North Norfolk Railway where it is undergoing full restoration to running order. The very last steam locomotive into Norwich was No 48752, a Stanier-designed 2-8-0 built at Brighton, allocated to the London Midland Region and fitted with a Stroudley whistle. It worked a cattle special from March to Norwich on 12 December 1963, covering for a diesel failure.

The last 'native' Norwich steamer to leave had been Class J17 No 65567, which went on 31 March 1962. However, some weeks after this official closure of the depot to steam, together with its banishment from the Ely-Norwich line, a chronic shortage of diesel power (accentuated by the very severe low temperatures of the 1962/3 winter) led to some 'B1s' in store at March being made serviceable. At least three and probably four of these were sent one night to Norwich, to be witnessed with some incredulity by a group of doctors returning home rather late from a social event at Wymondham. They were stopped by the gates at a level crossing, heard the whistle (the engines were travelling coupled together) and saw the convoy pass through. They knew that steam had officially ceased some time ago, and also that it had been an excellent party! One engine went to Lowestoft, another to Yarmouth, another to Ipswich, with one at Norwich. Although they were officially for carriage heating, one did cover a Cambridge turn.

Right:
Times change, and Class DJ12/2 No D2210 rests at Thorpe in April 1961. Note the Morgan's pub, swallowed up by Whitbread in the brewing holocaust of the late 1960s.
John C. Baker

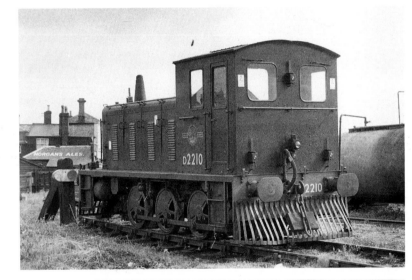

Right:
The last 'B12' at Norwich was No 61572. It had been officially due for withdrawal on 24 October 1960 but, for various reasons, stayed in active service for some time afterwards. When this photo was taken in May of the following year it was backing down on to its train prior to working to Sheringham.
John C. Baker

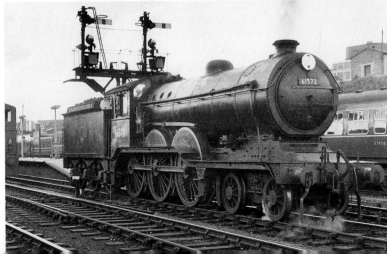

Right:
Class B17 No 61643
Champion Lodge
accelerates through
Whitlingham Junction with
an express in the early 1950s.
Dr Ian C. Allen

Below right:
Class B1 No 61252 heads
under Carrow Road bridge in
the late afternoon sunshine.
Dr Ian C. Allen

Below:
'Britannia' No 70013
Oliver Cromwell *is pictured*
in Norwich Thorpe during
April 1961. The remaining
Eastern 'Britannias' were
shortly to be transferred to
the London Midland Region
from where they were to be
eventually withdrawn. That
was not the end of the story
for No 70013 which was to
return to the area for
preservation after officiating
on the final BR main line
steam-hauled passenger
service in August 1968.
Notice in the background the
Derby Lightweight DMU.
John C. Baker

CHAPTER 8

Train Services

T
rain services to Norwich Thorpe have always been varied and interesting. Lines radiate from it to Yarmouth and Lowestoft, Cromer, Thetford and Ely, and Ipswich and London. It was the terminus for cross-country local trains from Dereham, Wells and King's Lynn, expresses from the Midlands and North as well as the Liverpool Street via Cambridge expresses. In the early 1920s a typical weekday would see some 30 trains to Lowestoft and Yarmouth, including through restaurant car workings to London and York. There would be about six trains to Dereham and Lynn, about a dozen to Cromer, again often carrying through coaches from London, and eight or nine trains to Liverpool Street via Ipswich, some fast and others rather less so, with slightly more via Cambridge; the former were much faster, with the Cromer expresses booked to take only just over $2^1/2$hr. There was also a good local service to Ipswich, with 14 intermediate stations open, including Trowse, instead of the present three. There were even five trains to Dereham via the 'round the world' line through Wroxham and Aylsham.

Wartime naturally took its toll, but after it was all over things got back to normal and timings started to be restored. The 1946 timetable showed the 6.40pm Liverpool Street express arriving at Norwich at 9.13pm, having called only at Ipswich, one of the best trains of the day. In 1951 all of the lines were still open for passengers, although Trowse station had closed in 1939. The summer timetable showed the first fruits of the new timings: the 8.30am down was scheduled to take only 2hr and 53min compared with the 3hr 12min of its predecessor, the 8.12am. Named trains had reappeared some time before, such as the 'Norfolkman', which now left at 9.30am and called only at Ipswich on its way to Norwich, where arrival was at 11.40am. It then continued to North Walsham, whence the main train with restaurant car went to Cromer High, and the remainder to Sheringham via Mundesley.

The train had been inaugurated on 27 September 1948 at Liverpool Street station, and as the *Eastern Region Magazine* commented: 'A unique feature of the inaugural ceremony of this train was that it was officially despatched from London by a provincial Mayor. Arrangements had been made for London's Lord Mayor to officiate and for the Mayor of Ipswich to travel with the train; also for the Lord Mayor of Norwich, Mr W. G. Cutbush, to meet the train on arrival at Norwich. At the last moment the Lord Mayor of London, Sir Frederick Wells, was unable to attend owing to an unfortunate indisposition and the honour of giving The Norfolkman its inaugural "right away" at 10.0am fell to the Mayor of Ipswich, Alderman J. B. Cunningham.' The Eastern Region saw the train as complementing the recently reintroduced 'East Anglian'; it either gave a 'night in London' or allowed London businessmen the chance to visit Ipswich or Norwich in a day, with reasonable time to conduct their business at either place. The return train left Norwich at 5pm, and reached London at 7.20pm. It was then typically hauled by one of the 'Bongos', the Class B1 4-6-0s, and consisted of eight coaches, with full reservation and restaurant

Previous page:
A Class 101 DMU departs from Thorpe amidst a cloud of exhaust with the 14.48 service to Great Yarmouth via Acle on 26 May 1982.
R. S. Freeman

facilities available in both directions, and did the journey to Norwich at an average of just over 51mph.

The rest of the 1951 express timetable had been similarly converted to departures at half-past the hour, and they were at 10.30am, 12.30pm, 1.30pm and 3.30pm to Cromer, the last being the 'Broadsman'. As with the 'Norfolkman', this went to Holt and Cromer High, with the train dividing at North Walsham. The 4.30pm was a Norwich train, and the 5.30pm a Cromer; the 7.30pm also terminated at Norwich. Between these, at 6.30pm, was the 'East Anglian', which had its beginning on 27 September 1937, when it was introduced to give a service on Mondays to Fridays between London and Norwich at an average speed of over 51mph. It was suspended for seven years because of the war, being reintroduced on 7 October 1946, using the same six coaches that had been specially designed by Gresley, and which had attracted so much interest when they first appeared. It was also seen as a train for businessmen, the up departure being at 11.45am from Norwich.

In the up direction, the service from Norwich had been similarly rearranged, with the 'Broadsman' at 7.45am, Cromers at 8.45 and 9.45am, the 'East Anglian' at 11.45am, a Melton Constable at 1.45pm, Norwich at 2.45 and 3.45pm, Cromer at 4.45pm, the 'Norfolkman' at 5.45pm (arriving in London at 7.55pm) and a Cromer at 6.45pm. The trains were now both heavier and faster, the best trains carrying nine or ten coaches instead of eight, and taking exactly two hours for the journey. On the other hand the 7.23pm all-stations to Ipswich connected there for London, now arriving as early as 12.7am!

There was much general goods traffic in and out of Norwich. In 1938 its value to the railway amounted to nearly £50,000, of which the largest amount was in iron & steel of various sorts, including consignments of scrap. Livestock featured very largely, helped by the cattle markets, and was the most valuable of all the traffics at over £10,000. Grain and flour were very important, and confectionery and preserves — mostly from Rowntrees — amounted to over 1,600 tons. Other traffics included round timber, wines & spirits and agricultural seeds.

Most of the Great Eastern traffic arrived via the Ely line, and it was handled at Thorpe, Trowse and Victoria, with the latter two tending to handle bulk goods such as coal and cement. Thorpe dealt also with the smaller wagonload items. As late as 1965 there was still a procession of nine trains every day from Whitemoor to one or other of the Norwich yards (Trowse, Wensum Junction, Thorpe), and including workings such as the 3.45am to Lowestoft Central, calling at Wensum Junction at 5.35am, or the 2pm to Lowestoft. Other workings included the daily 2.59pm Fawley to Hethersett tanks, arriving at 3.4pm, which worked back at 7.25pm, locomotives being serviced at Thorpe. The 4.18am from Ely to Thorpe called at Thetford and Wymondham, whilst the 1.58am from Thames Haven came in the same way. Traffic off the Wells and King's Lynn lines arrived via the 6.15pm from Dereham, whilst there was an arrival at 10.43pm from Cambridge at Wensum Junction.

Things were much the same in the up direction, with a few trains from Yarmouth Vauxhall and Lowestoft passing through non-stop. Three trains of empty wagons left for Whitemoor, the 4.30am from Trowse calling at all stations to Brandon, together with the 6.13pm empty petrol tanks to Cambridge, which ran as required. Additionally there were local goods trains to Lowestoft at 4.20am, 9.20am and 12.30pm, and to Yarmouth at 4.55am, 10.37am and 7.47pm. Trains ran out to Dereham at 4.45am and 9.13am; 10 years earlier there had also been workings to Cromer Beach at 5.20am, Wroxham at 8.35am to Wroxham and all stations to Cromer High, and all stations to Reepham at 9.37am.

Despatches towards London would be destined for Goodmayes or Spitalfields yards, or possibly Bishopsgate, although Temple Mills came to greater prominence in the 1950s. Because of the chronic lack of track capacity on the main line, especially between Colchester and Shenfield, most of the freight worked at night. For example, in 1955 there were the 10.3pm Spitalfields-Wensum Junction and the 11.45pm Goodmayes-Trowse, much of the traffic on both arriving via the London Docks, possibly raw materials for the big manufacturers such as Lawrence Scott or Boulton & Paul, or fruit and vegetables from the Continent and further afield. There were some daytime trains, some timed at quite high speeds, such as the 5.2pm Stowmarket-Trowse.

In the up direction trains were often timed to leave in the early evening and arrive in London in the small hours. One of the first to depart was the 3.10pm Class F to Spitalfields, calling at Goodmayes and Mile End, and arriving at 12.17am, whilst the 9.54pm Class D arrived at Goodmayes at 1.33am and Spitalfields at 2.19am. Much freight working had involved lodging turns, so that a Norwich crew might take a goods to Spitalfields one day, run light to Stratford and lodge, and return with a down working the following night. Even in the 1950s much of the still-extensive coal traffic was in unbraked wagons, which generated a huge amount of empty mileage to get them back to the pits. Local traffic was catered for by trains such as the 6.5am Class K from Ipswich, which called at Stowmarket, Finningham, Mellis, Diss and Tivetshall, arriving at Trowse at 12.58pm, having shunted them all on the way. It was balanced by the 1.40pm Class J all-stations to Ipswich. The epitome of the local goods train was undoubtedly the 3.15am from Thorpe, which called at and shunted all stations to Mellis, ran down to Eye, and finally reached Stowmarket at 12.47pm. A similar trip served the Waveney Valley line, and a 'J15' or 'E4' would leave with this at 8.4am.

Newspaper traffic was very important, being time-sensitive. In the 1949 timetable the 2.40am from Liverpool Street called at Manningtree and Ipswich, arriving at Norwich at 5.37am. It was turned over to 'Britannia' haulage right from their introduction, the locomotive having worked up on the 9.41pm Class D goods from Thorpe to Spitalfields. This had been a notoriously poor runner prior to the 'Britannias' arrival, but pride in the new locomotives cured the problem.

By the 1960s railway freight traffic was beginning to look much thinner. A feature in the Eastern Region Magazine in 1962 illustrated the density of traffic on different lines: although London-Haughley was carrying between 10,000 and 50,000 tons per week, Haughley-Norwich was down at 5,000 to 10,000 tons. The Beeching Report showed each of the Norwich stations (Thorpe, Victoria, Trowse and City) generating over 25,000 tons per annum, although many of the country stations were producing much less. Dr Beeching's answer was to close the smaller outposts and concentrate on 'railheads', of which Ipswich and Norwich were two of the few, and there was to be a service between them. Norwich, however, was to have a 'liner train' service from London — but from King's Cross, via Stevenage, Cambridge and Ipswich. The Class K goods was doomed!

Right:
On 29 August 1950 ex-GER 'J20' No 4696 — still unrenumbered and without its cast smokebox numberplate — is pictured leaving Norwich Thorpe goods yard with the 2.29pm Class F freight to Goodmaye's.
          E. Tuddenham

Below:
On 1 March 1958 No 70034 Thomas Hardy stands in platform 3 with the 2.42pm service to Liverpool Street via Ely, while in platform 4 No 70011 Hotspur heads the 2.45pm via Ipswich. A Derby DMU formed of cars Nos 79021 and 79613 waits in the centre road.
          Author's Collection

Right:
Class B1 No 61335 passes
Thorpe Junction with a
parcels train from Lowestoft
in 1960.
         Dr Ian C. Allen

Right:
Class D16/3 No 62511 heads
a Lowestoft-Norwich-
Dereham-Lynn-March
parcels trains under
Lakenham viaduct, probably
in 1957.
         Dr Ian C. Allen

Right:
Taken in 1960 from the
Carrow Road bridge, this
view shows 'J17' No 65567
drawing empty stock out of
the station. Behind the engine
is the diesel fuelling point
used by the DMUs, whilst
the lines to the left lead into
the goods depôt.
         Dr Ian C. Allen

Right:
Looking across the station throat towards Norwich Thorpe signalbox it is possible to see (nearest the camera) Class 31 No D5543 departing with the 4.20pm service for Liverpool Street on 16 September 1964. On the extreme left is the locomotive shed and, apart from other Class 31s, a Class 37 is also visible.
Stanley Creer

Right:
At Lakenham viaduct No D318 heads a short local train under the main line on a fine spring day.
Dr Ian C. Allen

Right:
Class 31 No 31408 departs from Norwich Yard with a mixed freight on 22 September 1982.
John Scrace

Right:
Class 47 No 47584 departs from Norwich with the 13.46 service to Liverpool Street on 22 September 1982. Visible in the distance, with locomotives of Classes 31, 37 and 47 present, is the locomotive shed. In the foreground is the DMU fuelling point.

John Scrace

Below right:
A dramatic view of the station throat at Norwich Thorpe in the era before electrification. A two-car Cravens-built DMU is seen leaving the station with the 13.50 service to Sheringham on 26 May 1982. A Class 47 is departing with a tank train and also visible are representatives of Classes 08 and 37.

R. S. Freeman

Below:
On 2 September 1989 a Class 37 arrives 'under the wires' at Thorpe station. The loss of the Thorpe signalboxes and the traditional semaphore signals means that the view from the platform end has radically altered over the past decade.

Brian Morrison

Right:
Class 31 No 31101 removes
the stock from Thorpe
following arrival from
London.
   John G. Glover

Below:
On 25 June 1975 Class 47/0
No 47170 arrives at Thorpe
with the 16.30 service from
Liverpool Street to
Yarmouth. Class 31 No
31158 waits to take the train
onwards to the east coast.
   Brian Morrison

Table 3 — LONDON (Liverpool Street), COLCHESTER, CLACTON-ON-SEA, HARWICH, IPSWICH, NORWICH, BECCLES, LOWESTOFT, and YARMOUTH

Week Days

A For particulars of London Suburban Service see Suburban Time Table.
b To Bury St. Edmunds Table 25
D Station for Cranpees Ash
L Via Lowestoft. One class only
S Saturdays only
U Buffet Car Liverpool Street to Norwich (Thorpe)
X or I One class only
B Third class only

B Arr 8.45 nrn
S Saturdays only
Clacton-on-Sea and Holland-on-Sea
d Arr 9.6 nrn

Table 3 — *Continued* LONDON (Liverpool Street), COLCHESTER, CLACTON-ON-SEA, HARWICH, IPSWICH, NORWICH, BECCLES, LOWESTOFT, and YARMOUTH

Week Days — *Contd.*

A For particulars of London Suburban Service see Suburban Time Table
b To Bury St. Edmunds (Tables 25)
c Clacton-on-Sea and Holland-on-Sea

D Station for Cranpees Ash
F or E Except Saturdays
L Via Lowestoft. One class only
S Sat. & Saturdays only
U Through Car
U Buffet Car Liverpool Street to Norwich
W Walton-on-Naze
Z Yarmouth (Southall) via Norwich (Thorpe)
B Third class only

Below:
The working timetable for freight services over the Norwich-Ely route c1960.

Below
The working timetable from the Norwich Thorpe-Sheringham line c1960.

Opposite page:
An LNER weekdays timetable for the London-Norwich Thorpe route.

K44 — WEEKDAYS — NORWICH TO ELY

UP				7*41	7*43	7*43	7*41	7*41	7*41	7*15	7*41
				23.08 Empties Norwich T. to Whitemoor	22.36 Lowestoft Cen. to Whitemoor	23.55 Trowse to Whitemoor	To Whitemoor	Empties to Whitemoor	Empties to Whitemoor	To Dereham	Empties to Whitemoor
Mileage M	C			MX	MX	MX	MO		MX		MO
0	0	NORWICH THORPE dep	1						4 30	4 45	5 10
		Wensum Jn. Sidings	2								
1	0	Trowse arr	3								
		dep	4			Same as page 45	1 20	2 45	4 36	4 51	5 16
6	15	Hethersett	5								
10	16	WYMONDHAM arr	6							5 12	
		dep	7			0 18	1 43	3 08	4 56	5 57	5 36
12	69	Spooner Row	8								
15	77	ATTLEBOROUGH arr	9						5 08		5 48
		dep	10	Same as page 45	Same as page 45	0 29	1 54	3 19	5 33		6 02
19	55	Eccles Road	11						R		
22	58	Harling Road	12						R		R
30	49	THETFORD arr	13		[5]				6 22		6 43
		dep	14	0 13	0 32	0 57	2 22	3 47	6 42		7 00
33	22	Two Mile Bottom	15						R		
37	63	BRANDON arr	16			1 12			7 09		7 18
		dep	17	0 27	0 46	1 31	2 36	4 01	7 35		7 35
41	49	Lakenheath	18								
46	72	Shippea Hill	19	0 44	1 03	1 51	2 53	4 18	7 55		7 55
52	33	Ely North Junction	20	0 55	1 15	2 04	3 04	4 30	8 06		8 06
53	64	ELY arr	21								
		dep	22								

UP		0-17	4-47	4-19	7*19	4-41	4-21J	4-21	4-21	4-41	4-21	0-17	7*60	4081
		LE	13.50 Yarmouth Vaux. to Whitemoor		To Whitemoor	To Whitemoor	To Cambridge	To Cambridge	To Cambridge	To Whitemoor	To Cambridge	LE	15.00 from Norwich City	To Fawley
		SX Q		SX			SX	SO	SO Q	SO	SX Q	SX SOQ	SX	SX SOQ
NORWICH THORPE dep	1					15 20	16 08	16 08	17 34	18 13	18 13	18‖24		
Wensum Jn. Sidings	2		14 23										18 50	
Trowse arr	3													
dep	4		14 26			15 25	16 13	16 13	17 39	18 18	18 18	18 28	18 56	
Hethersett	5				Lakenheath arr. 15.56 Shippea Hill arr. 16.20							18‖39		19 25
WYMONDHAM arr	6					15 43		16 31					19 17	
dep	7	14‖10	14 43			15 56	16 30	17 27	17 56	18 35	18 35			19 35
Spooner Row	8													
ATTLEBOROUGH arr	9	14‖23	Shippea Hill arr. 15D30			R			[1]		[1]			
dep	10		14 51			16 12	16 38	17 37	18 05 Conveys Empty Petrol Tanks	18 43	18 44 Conveys Empty Petrol Tanks			19 43
Eccles Road	11													
Harling Road	12						[5]		[5]		[5]	To work 19.25 to Fawley		
THETFORD arr	13					16 33	17 02							
dep	14		15 09			16 50	17 28	17 55	18 28	19 01	19 07			20 01
Two Mile Bottom	15													
BRANDON arr	16					R	17 40	18 05J	[2]		[2]			
dep	17		15 18		15 45	17 06	18 02	18 15	18 39	19 10	19 18			20 10
Lakenheath	18				16 06	[5]			[3]	[1]	[3]			[2]
Shippea Hill	19		15D36	16 10	16 25	17 24	18‖21	18 28	18 53	19 22	19 32			20 23
Ely North Junction	20		15 46	16 20	16*41	17 33	18 31	18 36	19 01	19 30	19 40			20 31
ELY arr	21			16 24			18 36		[5]		[4]			
dep	22						18 46	18 40	19 10		19 48			20 35

L34 — WEEKDAYS — NORWICH TO WROXHAM, REEPHAM, CROMER AND SHERINGHAM

Mileage M	C	M	C	DOWN		K	K	K	K	K	K	G	K
												LE	1.55 pm from Cromer High
						SX am	SO am	am	SX am	SX PM	SO am	SO PM	SX PM
				NORWICH THORPE	arr								
0	0				dep	5 20	5 58		8 35		8 35	After working 8.35 am from Norwich T.	
0	54			Wensum Jn. Sidings	arr	5 27	6 5		8 42		8 42		
					dep	5 50	6 25	9 37	9 51		9 51		
1	66			Whitlingham Jn.		5 57	6 32	9 44	9 58		9 58		
5	74			Salhouse	arr				10 12		10 12		
					dep				10 24		10 24		
8	60			WROXHAM	arr				10 36		10 36		
		0	0		dep	6 16	6 51	10 3	10 57		11 8		
		2	66	Coltishall	arr	To have additional engine attached N. Walsham Main to Cromer Beach after working 8.4 am from Sheringham		10 14					
					dep			10 34					
		5	46	Buxton Lamas	arr			10 45					
					dep			10 55					
		7	68	AYLSHAM SOUTH	arr			11 19					
					dep			11 42					
		13	16	Cawston	arr			12 6					
					dep			12 20					
		15	22	REEPHAM	arr			12 31					
13	2			Worstead	arr	R	R		11 15		11 26		
					dep				11 40		11 39		
15	77			NTH WALSHAM MN	arr	6 40	7 13		11 52		11 51		
		0	0		dep	9 4			12 35	12 57		12‖14	
		0	40	Antingham Road Jn.						1 0			
		3	39	Paston and Knapton						R			
		5	17	MUNDESLEY	arr					1 26			
19	61			Gunton	arr				12 50				
					dep	9 17			1X10			12 20	
23	25			Cromer Jn.	arr								2 0
		0	0		dep	9 28			1 24			12 27	2 1
23	79			CROMER HIGH	arr				1 29				
		0	51	Roughton Road Jn.		9 30						12 29	2 6
0	0	2	9	Newstead Lane Jn.		9X35						12X32	2 11
0	43			Runton East Jn.		9 37						12 34	2 13
1	20			CROMER BEACH	arr	9 41						12‖36	2 17
		2	60	Runton West Jn.									
		3	38	West Runton									
		5	15	SHERINGHAM	arr								
					dep								

Top:
A simultaneous departure during the
last years of steam out of Norwich sees
the last surviving 'B12' No 61572 heading
for Yarmouth and 'Britannia' No 70039
Sir Christopher Wren *setting off for Ely*
and the Midlands

Ian Allan Library

Above:
'Britannia' No 70002 Sir Geoffrey
Chaucer *is pictured leaving Thorpe with*
3.45pm Norwich-Liverpool Street service
on 1 September 1960

P.E.Moore

CHAPTER 9

Modernisation and Electrification

The beginning of the end for main line steam came in 1958, when the 2,000hp Type 4 diesel-electric locomotives began to be delivered by English Electric; they became better known in later years as the Class 40s. The first of them, No D200, made its demonstration run from Liverpool Street to Norwich on 18 April 1958 in the capable hands of Driver G. S. Marle, the train also carrying H. C. Johnson, Eastern Region General Manager. Ten of the new locomotives were allocated to the Eastern Region, and they were to be used on a proportion of the main Norwich trains, thus allowing the 'Britannias' to be released for the Clacton service. Local services had had the benefits of modern motive power for some time, with diesel railcars appearing from about 1954 onwards. Local services (along with many others) from Ipswich to Norwich were the subject of a major investigation into the economics of the new trains, and they were surveyed on two weeks, in March and September 1955. The line was one of the few where all its trains were included, so there were some interesting comparisons available between stopping, semi-fast and fast trains. In March, with the winter timetable in operation and local trains still steam-hauled, the fast trains showed gross receipts of £1,710 and movement costs of £764, giving an operating ratio of 45%. The respective figures for the semi-fast service were £1,816, £1,758 and 97%, whilst for the stoppers they were £496, £1,752 and a disastrous 353%. Train miles for the three types of service were respectively 1,890, 4,197 and 3,780. The summer service improved the operating ratio to 323% — hardly a worthwhile proposition. Closures of the local stations went on through the 1950s until only Stowmarket and Diss were left, although Needham later reopened.

Motive power changes on the main line were relatively insignificant for many years. Class 47 diesels replaced the Class 40s, and the service pattern settled down to hourly from Liverpool Street, alternate trains calling at Ipswich only, the others calling also at Manningtree, Colchester, Stowmarket and Diss. In the 1980s the extension of the electrification from Colchester was at long last resurrected, and with it came modernisation of the track and signalling. The first electric train to arrive in Norwich under its own power consisted of two four-car EMUs Nos 309622 and 309601, which ran from Stowmarket at 10.23am on 6 April 1987. The first passenger train ran on 9 April when No 86246 *Royal Anglian Regiment* hauled a special from Liverpool Street. There was a public preview on 5 May when the newly-named No 86220 *The Round Tabler* hauled another special, this time carrying local dignitaries, non-stop to Norwich in 83min 22sec, at an average speed of about 83 mph. The full electric service started on 11 May 1987.

A new depot was built at Crown Point, and the old Yarmouth & Norwich sheds were at last abandoned. The layout was remodelled and greatly simplified, with Thorpe station being closed over the Easter weekend in 1986. Trowse reopened briefly for passengers, a bus service being provided into Thorpe, and the exercise was repeated for the installation of the new signalling, now controlled

Previous page:
A four car Cravens set, with Class 105/2 leading, runs past Thorpe Station box as the 16.12 from Lowestoft.
Brian Morrison

from Colchester panel. This meant that all the Norwich signalboxes were abolished, the fringes becoming Whitlingham and Wymondham, although Crown Point depot was provided with its own miniature panel. Early in 1987 the 1905 swing bridge was replaced with a new single-track structure slightly upstream, the old one having become a bit too temperamental and liable to jam open in hot weather. It provided an interesting design problem for the engineers, who had to make sure that the overhead catenary also swung with the bridge. The layout at Trowse Lower junction was altered, so that instead of a traditional double junction the Ipswich line retained its double track, whilst a single-lead junction gave access to the older Thetford route. Trains were now able to use bi-directional signalling on all the approach lines, arriving or departing over either the up or the down roads.

Motive power changed again, Class 86 electric locomotives appearing on most trains, although occasional multiple units did appear; these also included converted EMUs for Post Office traffic. Norwich became part of the newly-formed Anglia Region, although the reorganisation into business sectors had already taken place, and these became supreme, the regions disappearing. It therefore came under the Provincial Sector, transformed after a couple of years into Regional Railways, Norwich and East Anglia being tacked on to their Central division, sitting uneasily with the West Midlands conurbation. Metro-Cammell Class 156 Sprinters arrived on cross-country services to Birmingham and Liverpool with the summer 1988 timetable, replacing trains of elderly BR Mark 1 or Mark 2a standard coaches hauled by Class 31 locomotives, and bringing improvements in frequency and speed, with the up-market Class 158 Express Sprinters arriving in 1991. This allowed the '156s' to be displaced on to local services, and they were joined by single-car Class 153s in 1993, themselves converted from the two-car Leyland-built Class 155s. This in turn allowed the replacement of the so-called 'heritage' multiple-units, mostly two-car Class 101s, although they were still to be seen covering occasional duties in the area through 1993.

Much change is heralded for the future, as reorganisation takes place in the run-up to privatisation, and liveries and rolling stock will certainly change again. Higher-density Class 150s have already replaced the Class 156s on local services, although this may not prove to be popular on some of the longer local runs. It may help to solve the bitter arguments over carriage of bikes, wheelchairs and the like, which have accompanied the Class 153s and 156s. The rest of the 1990s will certainly be an interesting time for railways everywhere in Britain, not just in Norwich — who knows, there may be a through Norwich to Paris service before the millennium is out! On a sadder note, early 1994 witnessed the demolition of the old Yarmouth and Norwich sheds, which just failed to survive until the 150th anniversary of that pioneering line.

78

Right:
*A fine view of Thorpe
Junction as Class 31 No
D5526 pulls out of the loop
with a freight from Yarmouth
to Norwich in March 1960.*
John C. Baker

Right:
*No D8205 is lurking by the
Carrow Road bridge, just
outside Thorpe Junction box
in March 1960.*
John C. Baker

Right:
*One of the many
experimental diesel
locomotives tried on British
Railways was No
D0280* Falcon, *seen here
leaving with an up service on
22 November 1961.*
Norfolk Record Office

Right:
An interesting view of the interior of the railcar depot, taken on 4 November 1971. The improvement in working conditions by comparison with the steam era is very obvious.
Eastern Counties
Newspapers

Right:
Looking towards Yarmouth, a DMU arrives from the coast on 27 November 1971.
H. W. Cater

Right:
Signalmen in Thorpe passenger yard signalbox pose for the camera on 23 February 1973. The cleanliness and state of the brightwork speaks for itself.
Eastern Counties
Newspapers

Right
Cravens two-car
unit arriving with an Ely
train on 26 June 1975 is
framed by the Carrow Road
bridge; the fuelling point can
be seen on the left. In the
background is Thorpe
Junction box.
                    Brian Morrison

Below:
Gloucester RCW Class 143
No E56100 leads Class 100
No E51114 on the 16.04 to
Yarmouth on 25 June 1975.
                    Brian Morrison

Right:
Much railway work is quite mundane, such as this short freight headed by No 03370 on 25 June 1975.
          Brian Morrison

Right:
Into the 1970s, and motive power has remained outwardly almost unchanged for a decade. No 31269 departs with the 17.55 Norwich to Ipswich parcels on a sunny 25 June 1975.
          Brian Morrison

Right:
With Crown Point yard in the background, a freight train comes out of Thorpe yard on 17 May 1966 and heads for Whitemoor.
                    Eastern Counties
                    Newspapers

Below:
A Birmingham RCW DMU passes Thorpe Junction with the 14.10 from Peterborough on 8 April 1978.
                    Les Bertram

Right:
On 18 June 1979 No 31183 passes Trowse station and Trowse Yard box with the 15.18 to Birmingham New Street.

C. F. Burton

Right:
Brundall signalbox is a block-built structure and controls the junction of the Lowestoft line with that to Yarmouth via Acle. Here the 09.35 from Yarmouth comes off the single-track line from Lingwood on 19 June 1979.

C. F. Burton

Right:
Brundall boasted two stops for Lowestoft and Yarmouth trains: Brundall Gardens halt, and Brundall station, the latter seen here looking east as a Cravens Class 105 calls at the up platform with the 14.29 Lowestoft to Norwich train on Saturday 22 August 1981.

Richard Lyndsell

84

Right:
Class 101, 120 and 105 DMUs pass the closed station at Trowse with the 11.02 local from Norwich to Peterborough on 8 August 1982.

John C. Baker

Right:
It is 31 July 1982 and Class 31s Nos 31102 and 31245 depart from Norwich under Lakenham viaduct and head towards Thetford with the Saturdays only 14.44 service from Great Yarmouth to Derby.

Dr L. A. Nixon

Right:
A view of the platform ends at Thorpe on 15 April 1982 with a Metro-Cammell unit on the 16.28 service to Yarmouth and a Cravens unit on the 16.14 service to Ely.

Michael J. Collins

Right:
In September 1983 a Class 47 heads past Trowse Yard signalbox and into the disused platforms at the closed station.

Brian Morrison

Below :
In pre-Sprinter days — March 1983 to be precise — Class 31 No 31405 passes Thorpe Junction en route for Thorpe station with the 08.04 from Birmingham New Street.

Alex Dasi-Sutton

ght:
view south from Norwich
orpe on 19 September
33 looking towards
orpe Station box. The old
gine shed is on the
reme right as No 47514
aits departure.

Peter Doel

low :
e complexity of Norwich
fore the electrification of
e station throat led to track
tionalisation. Apart from
e Class 31 departing on a
rvice westwards towards
eterborough, three Class
7s, a Class 37 and a Class
3 are also visible.

Brian Morrison

Above:
In the mid-1980s Norwich Thorpe was refurbished as part of the electrification programme. This shows the attractively repainted ticket hall, with the main train shed beyond.

British Rail

Right:
A classic view of Trowse swing bridge in April 1986, as No 45014 crosses with a freight for Whitemoor. Piling for the new bridge has just started.

R. J. Adderson

Class 47, No 47634
enry Ford, waits in the
atforms at Thorpe in
ctober 1986, with
ectrification masts recently
ected.

Terry Hewitt

ght:
r a brief but glorious
eekend at Easter 1986
owse station had its
ansong. Refurbished for
e occasion — the closure of
e throat at Thorpe for
modelling — all services
ere transferred there. Some
cals terminated, but many
n through to Yarmouth
d Lowestoft, and others
rned round at Brundall.
o 47582 County of
Norfolk *is in charge of a*
wn London.

R. J. Adderson

ight:
nd here to prove it really
d all happen — Trowse
rongs with people on its
cond and final reopening
1986. Permissive working
in force along platform 3,
ith Class 101s providing
cal connections.

R. J. Adderson

90

Right:
August 1988, and resignalling has been completed for some time, allowing the remaining manual boxes to be demolished. Thorpe Junction in its last moments as a Class 101 departs for Yarmouth.
R. J. Adderson

Right:
April 1987: the wires have recently been energised, and No 86246 Royal Anglian Regiment stands in Norwich Thorpe about to depart with a test run. Class 47 No 47513 and Class 31 No 31427 (failed) arrive with a service from Birmingham.
Bryan Newman

Right:
On 2 September 1989 Railfreight-liveried Class 47 No 47225 heads west towards Thetford with a rake of Network SouthEast-liveried coaches en route for Peterborough.
Brian Morrison

Right:
An interesting view of the new swing bridge from the track looking towards Trowse on 31 March 1988.

Brian Morrison

Below:
At Norwich Thorpe on 9 July 1990 a Parcels Sector unit, in Royal Mail red livery, headed by No 55994 with Class 114/1s Nos 54901 and 55931, awaits departure.

Brian Morrison

Right:

Right:

Photographed from the cab of a passing train on 9 July 1990, Class 156 'Super Sprinter' No 156412 forms the 12.45pm Norwich-Liverpool Lime Street service as it passes the south end of Crown Point depot en route towards Trowse.

Brian Morrison

Below:

On 27 October 1992 Parcels Sector EMU No 302991, in Post Office red livery, was seen in Thorpe. On the adjacent platform was Class 156 No 156407.

Brian Morrison

Above:
Electric trains between Liverpool Street and Norwich are now formed of 10 coaches with a Class 86 locomotive permanently coupled at the London end. At the Norwich end is a Driving Van Trailer (DVT) which has had its leading end converted to allow complete through control, thus obviating the need to run-round or use a turn-round locomotive at the termini, cutting the time spent there. On summer Saturdays some trains are extended from Norwich to Yarmouth, and since this section is not electrified a diesel locomotive is attached to the Class 86, the train being regarded as a fixed formation. Here, a Parcels-liveried Class 47 performs the duty near Whitlingham.

R. J. Adderson

Right:
Mails being loaded in platform 2 into a converted Parcels Sector DMU on 7 August 1990.
Adrian Vaughan

Right:
On 5 May 1987 the newly-named No 86220 The Round Tabler *is seen preparing to depart for London with a special train for members of the Round Table. It was later to achieve the return trip from London in just 83min 22sec!*
David C. Pearce

Right:
The classic shot taken from the Carrow Road bridge is brought into the age of the electric train as a Class 86 leaves Thorpe with a service for Liverpool on 11 November 1989. The lines of the station building can still be discerned, just, through a forest of catenary.
David C. Pearce

Right:
A Class 86 climbs away from Harford (Lakenham) viaduct with the evening 'Mail' on 4 May 1990. The vans are on the front of the regular passenger set. The train is pictured on the ascent out of the 'Dunston dip'.
David C. Pearce

Next page bottom:
A fine view of the concourse at Norwich Thorpe on 19 January 1991. Class 156 Sprinters are at the stops in platforms 2 and 3 waiting to work the 14.50 Lowestoft and 14.41 Great Yarmouth services respectively. An InterCity train, with a Driving Van Trailer leading, has recently arrived in platform 1.
David C. Pearce

Right:
Norwich Thorpe on 25 November 1989, with both a Class 86 and a Class 47 about to depart for London. The Class 86 is at the head of the head of the modern 'East Anglian'.
David C. Pearce